THE HEARTLAND INSTITUTE
59 EAST VAN BUREN, #810
CHICAGO, ILLINOIS 60605
(312) 427-3060

"Having been absent from the fighting, when I might have helped make possible the independence so dear to my countrymen, I set what skill and passion I can muster into this work, that it might inspire, that it might heighten the vitality of conscience so necessary to the realization of that Glorious Day when all are free."

—Eugène Delacroix, remarking on his masterpiece,
Liberty Leading the People, July 1830

SPECIAL ACKNOWLEDGEMENTS

Without the help of Thomas P. Westgaard and the Pine Tree Council, this project may have never been completed. I am grateful beyond words.

Also, I would like to thank David Y. Denholm, President of the Public Service Research Council, Washington, D.C., for his swift and faithful support.

Special thanks to:

>George and Joan Mueller
>B.D. and Francis Stebbins
>Dr. Jack Styles Kammer
>Ralph J. McClone
>Robert S. Asmuth
>John G. Hollingsworth
>Fred T. Kampo, Sr.
>Fred T. Kampo, Jr.
>Great Northern Corporation—Container Group
>Dr. Neal R. Kirkpatrick

Copyright © 1987 by Tobin James Mueller

All rights reserved. No part of this book may be reproduced or transmitted in any form or by any means, electronic or mechanical, including photocopying, recording, or by any information storage and retrieval system, without permission in writing from the Publishers, except for brief passages in connection with a review.

Mueller, Tobin James, 1955-
  The New Age Politics
  Cover subtitle: A contemporary declaration of life, liberty, and the pursuit of dignity.
  Bibliography: p.
  1. Liberty. 2. Rights theory 3. Ethical foundations of political freedom.
Library of Congress Catalog Card Number 87-71698
ISBN 0-942495-01-2

Printed in the United States of America

Front cover: A detail from Delacroix's
"Liberty Leading the People"

THE NEW AGE POLITICS

a contemporary declaration of Life, Liberty, and the Pursuit of Dignity

BY

TOBIN JAMES MUELLER

Amherst Press
A Division of Palmer Publications, Inc.
318 N. Main Street   P.O. Box 296
Amherst, WI 54406

To my father

*who has juggled the problems of life with dexterity rarely witnessed
in this Age of Forgetfulness
by living within his History yet mounting his own Future
all in the same motion.*

THE
NEW
AGE
POLITICS

Table of Contents
THE NEW AGE POLITICS

Author's Preface iv

PART ONE: SELF-RESPONSIBLE MAN

Introduction 1

Freedom and the Ethics of Aspiration 2
   Freedom as a Positive Concept 2
   "Freedom" - Not Always What It Seems 3

The History of Freedom 6
   Democracy's Tension: Liberty verses Equality 12
   Socialism and the Chains of the Collective 15
   Salvation Politics and the Yoke of Faith 18
   Humanism and a Unified World Order 23

Life, Liberty, and the Pursuit called Human Dignity 28
   The Relationship between Politics and Ethics 29
   The Search for a Politics of Selfestness 31
      (1) The Politics of Selflessness.. 31
      (2) The Politics of Selfishness... 32
      (3) Politics Beyond Ethics.. 34
      (4) The Need for a New Ethic... 35
      (5) Selfestness as a Comprehensive Ethical Concept......... 35
      (6) The Three Pillars of the New Age Politics.................. 36

PART TWO: SOVEREIGNTY AND ASSOCIATION

Introduction 38

Voluntary Association 40
   A "Sovereign Self" Defined 40
   Sovereignty's Explicit Clarification: Self-ownership 41
   The Libertarian Extension: Recognition of Sovereignty
      in Others.. 41
   The Need to Belong 44
   Pluralistic Community 48

PART TWO: SOVEREIGNTY AND ASSOCIATION (cont.)

Self-defense as Positive Force 56

Justice 59
   Justice as Independent of God and Nature 59
   Justice as a Human Concept 60
   Justice as Independent of Social Evolution and
      Capitalism 61
   Law and the "Order of Consonance": Giving Justice
      Political Coherency 64

PART THREE: THE POLITICS OF RIGHTS

Introduction 67

The Concept of Rights 73
   Rights and Well-being 73
   Rights and the Moral Individual 79
   Rights: An Extension of "Ultimate Value" 80
   Property: An Extension of Self-ownership 82
      Property Rights and Free Trade 86
   Property Rights as Basic Right 87
      Property Rights and Property Dispersal 89

The Allocation Principle 92
   The Allocation Process 94
   As a Test: Some Examples 94
   Limitation and Structure 98

Spontaneous Consonance 99
   Social Order as Common Sense 100
      (1) Duty and Subservience 101
      (2) Rational Agreement 102
   Society and Government as Separate Entities 103
   "Society as Criminal" Creates Need for Political Action 106
   Free Trade: Commerce as Needs Satisfaction 108
   Needs Satisfaction vs. Legislative Mandates 112
   The Family 116
      The Concept of Trusteeship 118
      Property Rights and the Transfer of Trusteeship 120

PART THREE: THE POLITICS OF RIGHTS (cont.)

Proper Attributes of Political Associations 123
   The Allocation Principle and Rights Protection 123
   Isonomy: Equality of Law 124
   Predictability 126
   No Monopoly Powers 128
   Representation and Balance 136
   Restitution, Not Punishment. 140
   Liability, Not Immunity 142
   Noncoercive Revenue 143
   In Conclusion 147

Practicality and Progress 149
   Ignorance and Liberty 152
   Exploitation and Regulation 155
   Taming the Beast with Required Compensation 161
   The Free Life - The Good Life 164

Selected Bibliography 167

AUTHOR'S PREFACE

The majority of the modern world is frightfully confused. It erroneously equates Social Democracy with self-sovereignty, political stability with societal success, relative prosperity with economic freedom, religious piety with ethical living, patriotic duty with personal fulfillment, and social respectability with rationality. It has lost its vision of a continuing human renaissance. It has lost its capacity for radical criticism. It has stumbled from the once widening course of constructive individualism.

The modern world has lost its sense of self-responsibility.

But the twentieth century, with its penetrating confusion and coercive excesses, was born out of an enlightened ethical mandate of personal sovereignty, a revolutionary renaissance of human self-determination that longed to burst the many chains of tyranny. Amidst its newspeak political jargon and its deafening philosophical cry for egalitarian altruism, our world still retains the seeds of a continuing struggle for human dignity. It is not a struggle meant to constrict and destroy, as has been displayed in recent wars and repressive regimes, but one meant to free the individual so that he could build. And it is from this creative and self-responsible tradition that THE NEW AGE POLITICS emerges.

Government, to the modern reformer, is the great apparatus of social sculpturing, an omnipotent machinery needing only an inspired leader to set it upon mankind and accomplish, in a few strokes, a handsome and complete work of art. But mankind is no longer made of clay. Man is flesh and blood and internally generated. He has discovered his individuality. He has entered a New Age, an age in which he self-consciously strives to fulfill the promise of his own individual integrity. Yet, this quest seems eternally damned as he drowns within his traditional tools of collective action: the institutions of hierarchy, of privilege, of subservience.

The pursuit of the dignity of human living requires a certain kind of progress, both on an individual level and on a social level. This progress can be defeated by the inertia inherent in both isolating selfishness and servile selflessness. It is tragically misdirected within the self-inflating institutions of modern government. A new path of progress must be forged - a universal flourishing of human dignity that is possible only when constructive individualism is nourished within a supportive, consentaneous human community. It is the purpose of this book to identify the rules these associations must maintain and, in doing so, ascertain the proper role of political activity within this dynamic, consonant order.

Such a challenge has been the continuing goal of New Age Man. My hope is that this book is able to add to this quest, by funnelling the great energy and wisdom of both the conservative and liberal traditions, recognizing the pertinence of related disciplines, from economics to psychology, and extending the discussion with a new spark, a common relevance, and a relentless demand for universal human dignity.

Man's oldest and most enduring symbol is the child: growing and free, ever on the verge, striving to come into his own. This is the greatness of man: the impassioned, audacious, aspiring, and innocent pursuit of his individual human potential. It is this quest that THE NEW AGE POLITICS seeks to continue.

Tobin James Mueller
4 July 1987

Part One:

SELF-RESPONSIBLE MAN

Part One:
SELF-RESPONSIBLE MAN

In order to develop a proper context in which to discuss contemporary political philosophy, with its dual agenda of individual liberty and social justice, we must first identify the historical roots of our many interpretations of "freedom" and define the legitimate role of ethics in politics. Therefore, Part One: SELF-RESPONSIBLE MAN will first introduce and later analyze the concept of freedom, arrriving at a definition which is consonant with certain ethical mandates. Second, the relationship between ethics and politics will be discovered, with special attention paid to the political consequences of major contemporary moral stances.

But SELF-RESPONSIBLE MAN is really only an introduction. The proper rules of social interaction must be made explicit. This is the purpose of Part Two: SOVREIGNTY AND ASSOCIATION. From this comprehensive base, a true POLITICS OF RIGHTS can be identified (Part Three), forming the concluding centerpiece of THE NEW AGE POLITICS.

SELF-RESPONSIBLE MAN, contains the following sections:

Freedom and the Ethics of Aspiration
    Freedom as a Positive Concept
    "Freedom" - Not Always What It Seems

The History of Freedom
    Democracy's Tension: Liberty verses Equality
    Socialism and the Chains of the Collective
    Salvation Politics and the Yoke of Faith
    Humanism and a Unified World Order

Life, Liberty, and the Pursuit called Human Dignity
    The Relationship between Politics and Ethics
    The Search for a Politics of Selfestness
        (1) The Politics of Selflessness
        (2) The Politics of Selfishness
        (3) Politics Beyond Ethics
        (4) The Need for a New Ethic
        (5) Selfestness as a Comprehensive Ethical Concept
        (6) The Three Pillars of New Age Politics

FREEDOM AND THE ETHICS OF ASPIRATION

Freedom as a Positive Concept

No other issue has been more ubiquitous in the modern age than freedom. It is individual freedom which *defines* the modern age, setting it apart from earlier ages of religious authoritarianism, hierarchical feudalism, and totalitarian monarchies.

In fact, freedom has become nearly synonymous with man himself. Without a context of freedom, the very definition of man becomes hollow and uninformative. How could we define man without *free will* or *self-determination*? How could we define human maturity without *self-reliance* or *personal conscience*? Is it not the power of human aspiration that forms the essence of freedom?

On the deepest level, freedom conceptualizes both the power and precariousness of man: he is a being who is utterly free to choose, yet who cannot escape the consequences of his eternally fallible choices. From this exhilarating yet sobering insight, man both clings and flees. But he can never escape this inherent self-responsibility.

Political philosophy must not ignore this fact. Freedom is more than a negative concept, more than the state of being free of control (as the civil libertarians would have it) or being free of want (as the socialists try to persuade). With reference to human consciousness and action, freedom is a positive assertion of individual dignity, the developed power of effective self-determination: it is a statement of man as a moral agent, of **self-responsible man**.

Because man aspires, because he desires a greatness beyond the status quo, he requires freedom. This heroic urge is an ethical sense; a desire for self-worthiness that necessarily breaks the chains of conformity. Without this urge, morality holds no appeal above the level of regulatory egalitarianism. Without an ethics of aspiration, personal liberty becomes an aimless vanity.

Heroic aspiration is essential to sustaining personal liberty in a democracy. Indeed, it has been the primary component within the American Spirit nourishing our desire for political freedom. No other ethical tendency can sustain the comprehensive powers of self-determination required by Self-responsible Man. The direct relationship between freedom and the ethics of aspiration cannot be overlooked;

upon the positive assertion of individual human dignity and purpose is built the only legitimate political argument for true personal freedom.

"Freedom" - Not Always What It Seems

The urge for freedom is common to us all, yet it is a source of tragic conflict as well. Beneath its banner people gather together in peaceful cooperation; beneath its banner people clash in violent revolution. It is a word used by advocates of reason - for reason demands the autonomy of the mind, while the mind demands autonomy of action. And it is used by advocates of happiness and spontaneity - for in the experiences of happiness and spontaneous action the raw recognition of being alive, of being self-sovereign, of being worth the effort, can be glimpsed. It is also used by the powerful to solidify their power over their subjects, equating freedom with license and domination.

What does freedom mean?

Nearly every contemporary political theory advocates freedom. Marx spoke of freeing the worker from the alienation of mechanistic labor and the exploitation supposedly inherent in capitalism. Herbert Marcuse, Marx's popular apostle, sought to free man from the deadening effects of consumerism and the one-dimensional mass culture. Both writers recognized the frailty of free men and sought an ethical society in which the evolution of human dignity would find no obstacles. Their mistakes were many, but the greatest among them was to make men means to an end instead of freeing men to determine their own ends. As a result, they demanded not freedom, but slavery.

Religious fundamentalists the world over seek to free men from temptation and the immoralities of liberal western tolerance. They seek an order based on ancient scriptures and a petrified morality. A single virtue is required: absolute faith in the leaders who dispense the One Blinding Truth. They recognize man's desperate need for morality yet render him incapable of acting ethically, denying man's ability to make moral choices based on human knowledge and autonomous judgment. As a result, they demand abject submission instead of authentic moral responsibility.

Social Democrats speak as if they were the single source of freedom. Indeed, greater freedom exists within the western democracies (relative to their eastern socialist counterparts), but that may be more an outgrowth of the revolutionary effects of liberalizing capitalism than a consequence of state-sponsored rights protection. The omnipotence of government authority has barely been altered since the days of Louis XIV; it is just that popular referendum has replaced ordained monarchy.

> The avowed difficulty is that democracy, no less than monarchy or aristocracy, *sacrifices everything to maintain itself* and strives, with an energy and a plausibility that kings and nobles cannot attain, to override representation, to annul all the forces of resistance and deviation, and to secure, by Plebiscite, Referendum, or Caucus, *free play for the will of the majority*. The true democratic principle, that none shall have power over the people, is taken to mean that none shall be able to restrain or to elude its power. The true democratic principle, that the people shall not be made to do what it does not like, is taken to mean that it shall never be required to tolerate what it does not like. The true democratic principle, that every man's free will shall be as unfettered as possible, is taken to mean that the free will of the collective people shall be fettered in nothing. . . Democracy claims to be not only supreme, without authority above, but absolute, without independence below; to be its own master, not a trustee. (Lord Acton, "Sir Erksine May's *Democracy In Europe*")

The state, sometimes by popular demand and sometimes in spite of it, confiscates over half of one's labor through taxes, controls all property through eminent domain laws, pervasive regulation, and outright state-ownership, and oversees nearly all aspects of education and employment. Personal freedom continues to be granted by state authority. Duty is still touted as the highest social virtue. In the end, what is left is a rather compromised definition of freedom, supercede by the omnipresence of democratic government.

"Freedom" - Not Always What It Seems

Around the globe it is the age-old tragic story, from the Soviet "Union" to "liberated" Mozambique, from starving Ethiopia to ravaged Cambodia, from the "Holy" Islamic Republic of Iran to the holier-than-thou tyrants of Central and South America. During a century that has witnessed cruelty unsurpassed in all of history, governments have outstripped the combined effort of their bloody wars (which tallied approximately 35 million deaths) by murdering, starving, and enslaving 172 million of their own citizens.

So much for state-sponsored human dignity.

The citizens of the New Age no longer wish to be subjects, whether under a dictator or a congress. They wish to be equal partners, bonded by a reverence for individual aspiration, not a fear of coercion. They want freedom to be a positive force of cooperative construction, not an excuse for individual sacrifice or a license for collective injustice.

To this end, our Founding Fathers invented a Land called America. It was to be an island without a national righteousness, without a required religious creed, without a centralized authority, without state-sponsored meaning. It was to be a land of potential, whose single beacon and single promise was self-sovereignty: the right of each individual to assert his individual dignity in every phase of living. Immigrants came here, not to become subjects of a benevolent government, but simply to be themselves, unfettered and unafraid. We find ourselves in its midst, wondering where the dream has gone.

This Land of Freedom is what the New Age demands.

THE HISTORY OF FREEDOM

Citing the intellectual roots of modern liberty, Gilbert Murray stated:

> It is worth noting that the idealization of Freedom is somewhat peculiar to the Hellenic or European tradition. You do not find much about it in, for instance, the Hebrew or Egyptian or Chinese tradition. The word *Liberalis* is derived from *Liber*, a free man, and means "like a free man", or "with qualities of a free man." The Greek ideal from which it was taken used simply the word "free." It is an ancient word and has, I freely admit, certain ancient, aristocratic associations about it. A Free Man must not stoop to certain ways of behaviour, such as cowardice, lying, meanness, stupidity. They are beneath him, slavish. He must resist all tyranny, whether foreign or home-grown. That is obvious. But the ideal of Freedom was specially taken up and developed in another sense by the Greek philosophers, who were fond of pointing out how few men are really free. Is a drunkard or a madman free? Obviously not; he is the slave of his craving or his delusion. A tyrant? No, he is always a slave of his passions or his fears. Men are slaves of their passions, customs, most of all perhaps their greed..., [lust] for power. . ., and prejudice [of what is new and different].

He clarified by adding:

> The constant struggle for freedom, the vigilance, the determination never to forget the duty of keeping the soul of man free, is perhaps more important, and certainly more inspiring, than the mere possession of freedom itself. To be merely free is not much. To be able to do whatever you want to do does not in itself produce a good life or a fine character. All you can

say is that without freedom the real problem of a good life cannot even begin. (*The Meaning of Freedom*)

Social and economic freedom devoid of moral virtue is a hollow sort of freedom, one which has little purpose. It is true that without freedom, virtue becomes impossible. A coerced act cannot be a virtuous act (or an immoral one, for that matter). There can be no virtue without the freedom of autonomous judgment and self-responsible experience. Freedom, to aid man, must be an expression of responsible choice, of moral agency, not merely an aimless assertion of will. For the Greeks, freedom cleared the way for the otherwise impossible pursuit of Socratic self-knowledge and Aristotelian strength of character.

Murray concludes by quoting Thucydides; "The secret of happiness is freedom, and the secret of freedom is courage."

The original ideal of Freedom was not merely the absence of compulsion. It was the state of being sufficiently self-controlled so that the *good life*, the happy life, the life of self-fulfillment could be pursued. It took work, civilizing and introspective work, and courage in the face of internal inertia, rampant self-deception, and myriad societal pressures for conformity. Freedom was merely a means to an end: the satisfied self.

In the area of political freedom, the Greeks began to secularize the state by placing judicial emphasis on human judgment and steering away from ancient connections between gods and law. This is how democracy was born. Once the human aspect of self-determination was recognized, the democratic forum, wherein each citizen had an equal voice, became the natural mechanism to replace autocratic theocracy. In the sphere of human interaction, the appropriate standard was individual conscience, not the pronouncements of oracles or their professional interpreters. Just as the very concept of "mind" was emerging as a personal possession, a distinctly human entity, no longer considered a mere extension of divine communication (and, in this way, secularized as well), so to did political apparatuses reflect the emerging individuality of men no longer viewed as mere puppets of playful gods. The secularized state set the stage for a wide range of mechanisms that would come later, all designed to protect individual conscience, all grounded in the notion that law was an expression of an individual's natural right to pursue, rationally, his own well-being.

Hellenic Freedom, however, was not well protected. Political activity was often a matter of aristocratic-democratic whim, of majority vote, of spontaneous and often passionate group decision. It wasn't until the Roman concept of strictly codified administrative law became wedded to this ideal that, for the first time, politically *protected liberties* became a possibility. Roman citizens were not to be subjected to the whim of a spontaneous mob or an overzealous local official. Law was to be the voice of order and the only sanctioned wielder of force. The administration of law was to be conducted with detached correctness and calm authority. And because laws were written down and codified, men could plan for them. A rational expectation framework could be incorporated into one's daily and long term affairs.

The rule of Roman Law brought an unprecedented period of peace to Europe. It matured the idea of Freedom into one which could be supported by a political structure. But Roman Law was not entirely consistent with Hellenic Freedom. It was still a legislative prerogative, not a natural right. Duty (social, political, religious) consistently came before personal well-being. Sovereignty, ultimately, was still in the hands of those who wrote the laws, not inherent in each man by right. Also, Roman Law was never universal; the ancient scourge of slavery continued to be sanctified by law and religion. It was not long before the Roman Republic was propelled past demagogical democracy into simple dictatorship.

During this time, the Hellenic vision of personal well-being was being extended by Epicureans, Aristotelians, and others who recognized the self-determined nature of human consciousness. Most influential, however, was the growing concept of individual immortality and the individualistic belief that a specific soul could construct for itself its own destiny. Self-made destiny was a natural extension of the Hellenic idea of *psyche* and self. Christianity, a religion that acknowledged the individuation of each human spirit, its importance *as an individual* before God, and placed the power of salvation within the realm of free will, succeeded in augmenting the importance of self-responsibility. Early Christian communities also delimited the sphere of the secularized state by demanding that *all* matters of soul and conscience be outside of Caesar's reach.

Christianity, however, was not without its sinister inconsistencies. The majority of Christian dogma placed the freeing element squarely in the hands of God, thus robbing man of any substantive role in Ultimate Destiny. Christianity also relied on the nonrational concept "faith" as the fundamental means for discovering the good life. Man too easily became God's sheep in affairs of conscience and Government's sheep in socio-political matters. In many ways, the Christian interpretation of Freedom completely reversed the Hellenic insistence upon self-determined soul. And by making reason subservient to faith, it further eroded the domain and effectiveness of man's cognitive potential. The individualistic interpretation of self-responsible soul still remains a problematic inconsistency within Christianity's foundation of faith, predetermination, and complete obedience to the One Almighty.

On the political level, the Christian Church inherited, through Constantine, the immense bureaucracy and excessive totalitarianism of the late Roman Empire. In fact, it might be more accurate to insist that Catholicism was the enduring legacy of the Roman Empire. The Church utilized the seasoned mechanisms of hierarchical stratification, entrenched bureaucracy, and centralized authoritarianism to quickly expand its spheres of influence. The result transformed the humble words of Christ into an institutional ethic that put Church above individual well-being, dogma above personal salvation, commandment above truth.

Once the Church was armed with the awe-inspiring power of an omnipotent state, it was able to legitimize social intolerance, castrate intellectual pursuit, stilt or reverse all ethical progress in the name of scriptural righteousness, and aggressively disseminate its narrow definition of Absolute Truth. The "virtues" of duty and faith combined to create a fundamentalist utopia. The affect was to throw civilization into irresponsible moral darkness: the Age of Faith.

(This "darkness" was not a necessary outgrowth of the Christian message, however. Christianity's association with State Power and Legislative Prejudice had a great deal more to do with the Church's medieval excesses and the atrocities committed by colonial powers in the name of religion than any aggressive intolerance appearing in the New Testament. It is the nature of government to abuse humanity; all ideologies are sullied by intimate association with it.)

The Enlightenment brought with it the promise of greater consistency. Reason was again viewed as the freeing principle in men's lives. In a way, this was a return to the Aristotelian concept of rational man, but the philosophers of the Enlightenment were more comprehensive in their arguments, augmenting ethics and theology with psychological, political, and economic reasoning. Man was seen as able to control his own destiny *without any recourse to the supernatural.* Mind and reason were recognized as man's most powerful and virtuous characteristics. Reason was understood as the tool man must employ in order to harness the world for his own benefit. Each man was to make his life in the image of *his own potential.*

Politically, individual pursuits were to be protected by the mechanisms of conservative republicanism. The English did not wish to break with the past (as the French liberals later attempted), but merely make their present order more responsive. Therefore, they based the structure of representative government on the imperial model, with professional politicians assuming the responsibilities of their already stratified society: the central monarch, the hereditary aristocratic, and the small land owner. Thus, in many ways, Republican Government gave popular sanction to an imperial-institutional ethic and assisted the status quo in resisting change. Supposedly aligned with society's best interests, the Enlightened State was more often just as removed and contrary to the interests and universal rights of individuals as was the monarchy it replaced.

More important than Republican Government was the liberalized system of voluntary commerce that evolved. From the expanding notion of Enlightenment Freedom came a social structure of economic self-interest disciplined by individual rights. Within it, law was to be supreme, but not a state-sanctified version of Roman Law. Individual people were viewed as the sovereigns of their individual lives, not the subjects of states or generals or barons, popes or bishops or priests, national coalitions or local communities or specialized guilds. Men were to have a right to own their own lives and labor, their own property and time, their own thoughts and opinions. The Enlightenment stressed that a system of voluntary commerce was the best environment in which these rights could be maintained, a system later termed "capitalism" because it enable an individual to possess and invest his own capital in any way he saw fit - within the law of natural individual rights. Capitalism further "secularized" Freedom by establishing a socio-economic system which was autonomous of the centralized planning and capricious interventions of state action. Force was to be outlawed, replaced by contractual consent. Compulsion was to be abolished, replaced by mutual benefit. Freedom was expanded to encompass nearly all aspects of human interaction.

But the problem of proper human motivation did not seem to be satisfactorily answered by capitalism. In the 1800s, capitalism was frequently defended because it created wealth so effectively; it did not, however, provide any ethical vision or social continuity for the community. It was sometimes defended as a way for people to serve society, in the Christian-altruistic tradition, by making businessmen a socially useful mechanism in terms of *aggregate prosperity*; sometimes defended as a means of serving God and avoiding temptation, in the Christian-Calvinist tradition, by continual toil and productive penance. Rarely was it defended as a socio-economic system which had the potential for creating virtuous people or a cooperative, law-abiding nation. Far from being an entrepreneurial giant pursuing a Socratic concept of integrity and intelligent living, the capitalist individual was more often portrayed as an isolated, selfish cut-throat whom society endured mainly because he was so good at making a profit. Virtue, on the other hand, was increasingly generalized into collective need, epitomized by the concept of Social Will.

Law gradually became a supportive mechanism of this Social Will, reversing an earlier emphasis on the protection of the individual through contract law and property rights. Such a philosophical shift was viewed as progress toward an ideal of complete social justice. Socialism was born. It seemed to answer the problem of motivation: Why do you do things? For the good of all. Why do you work hard? To fulfill the needs of the many. Why do we make laws? To socially engineer the Good Society. Marx's maxim, "from each according to his ability, to each according to his needs," summed up the perfect altruistic community.

Concepts which had long been distorting the true essence of Freedom now began to destroy it altogether.

Freedom became, politically, a secondary concern. Since Rational Man supposedly had the power to create, through reasoned law, any social system he might envision, his first priority became the political engineering of society. Create a utopian society and you will have, automatically, Utopian Men. Socialism re-sanctified the state, making it the sacred (yet secular) instrument through which all men would achieve salvation.

What went unproposed was an ethical philosophy that grounded individual freedom within a truly universal concept of human dignity. What was forgotten was that the definition for the "good life" was to be entirely self-made by each individual. What went undefended was the psychological source of man's self-determination: what might be termed man's freedom-as-personal-consciousness. What was ignored was man's vast ignorance and the actual limits of reasoned political effectiveness: leaders' inability to plan, to the last and needed detail, a utopian society of any kind. What was rationalized away was self-responsibility. What became impossible was human fulfillment.

By socialism I do not mean merely a partisan socialistic political theory. My usage here connotes a *socialistic ethic* or a code of values which surrenders individual aspirations to collective opinion, which places social rankings such as class, race, position, or party before personal sovereignty, and which replaces authentic ethical inquiry with centralized intolerance and sloganeering.

Even after the socialist ethic was responsible for the establishment of blatantly oppressive and expansionist states in National Socialist Germany and the Union of Soviet Socialist Republics (thus, it would seem, discrediting the political theory of socialism to all but a few die hards), the underlying "ethical" doctrine of socialism has remained relatively untouched. It has become (1) the major motivation for most democratic legislation; (2) the rationalization for modern dictatorship; (3) the favored social ethic for most religious world organizations; and (4) the utopian vision for most democratic humanists. Let us examine this phenomenon so to better understand its probable consequences.

Democracy's Tension: Liberty vs. Equality

Alexis de Tocqueville compared democracy to socialism 150 years ago and came upon the following conclusion:

> Democracy extends the sphere of individual freedom; socialism restricts it. Democracy attaches all possible value to each man; socialism makes each man more an agent, a mere number. Democracy and Socialism have nothing in common but one word:

Democracy's Tension: Liberty versus Equality

equality. But notice the difference: while democracy seeks equality in liberty [the equality of rights under the law], socialism seeks equality in restraint and servitude...all leveled by coercion to a single class. (*Democracy In America*)

Times have changed. Democratic people, of the so-called free world no longer consider equality in terms of universal personal sovereignty. They no longer consider it the task of their democratic institutions to merely protect individual liberty (and, perhaps, they never did). They now consider it a human right to have government supply them directly with everything from "free" education to comprehensive retirement plans. They consider it their civil right to have government force employers to supply them with jobs, to hire on the basis of quotas instead of ability, to be constantly regulated so free market competition does not "hurt" those who cannot keep up or who are in a "nongrowth" industry. They think it a proper extension of democratic liberty to control another's property through zoning laws, rent control, and the governmental practice of eminent domain. They think it their moral duty to control another's private interests through invasive ordinances against noncoercive private activities. In the name of the social welfare, they believe no woman or man should be able to work without governmental *permission*, without a proper certificate or license. In short, they consider it the job of democracy to *create* the Good Society, not simply to supply a free and equitable context in which individuals make their own good life.

Equality no longer means "equality of justice under the law." Rather, it now connotes "sameness of the human condition." Equality of Opportunity, meaning the freedom to pursue one's own life-goals, has lost out to Equality of Results, meaning that everyone must begin and end at the same level (no matter how much state-sanctified violence is required to achieve that unnatural result).

Political Freedom no longer means being left alone, left to one's own devises, so that the good life can be pursued (as in Jefferson's "life, liberty and pursuit of happiness"). It is no longer synonymous with self-responsibility. It now means "freedom *from* failure," in other words: security, aid, paternalism, protectionism. Liberty once fought the battle for individual rights, but socialism's concept of equality has won out.

> The subtle change in the meaning to which the word freedom was subjected in order that this argument should sound plausible is important. To the great apostles of political freedom the word had meant freedom from coercion, freedom from arbitrary power of other men, release from the ties which left the individual no choice but obedience to the orders of a superior to whom one was attached. The new freedom promised, however, was to be a freedom from necessity, release from the compulsion of circum- stances which inevitably limit the range of choice of all of us, although some very much more than others. Before men could be truly free, the "despotism of physical want" had to be broken, the "restraints of the economic system" relaxed. (F. A. Hayek, *The Road to Serfdom*, chapter entitled "The Great Utopia")

Freedom is no longer a staunch ally of de Tocqueville's "democratic equality"; it has become an excuse for political compulsion. Freedom is no longer a crusading *protector* of the individual against "socialistic equality"; it has become *synonymous* with "socialistic equality" - or, more accurately, it is the active force which is meant to free a people from all but socialistic organization. Freedom is no longer "individual liberty"; it has become "governmental liberty."

Perhaps this transition becomes more understandable if democratic mechanisms are viewed in a more realistic light then that employed by de Tocqueville. Democracy's actual definition of freedom might be translated "the voluntary deferment of an individual's rights to the legislative prerogative of his elected officials for the good of the General Will." Although the Republic of the United States, for example, attempts to pit the interests of various factions within the General Will against each other, so to better insure the accountability of government to "the People," this usually translates into legislation that merely increases the power of those groups which have the most to offer legislators in turn. Democracy then collapses into a Politics of Legislative Buy-out. The General Will becomes a compromise between an oligarchy of legislators and their specific backers.

Democracy is a creature of popular opinion. In the struggle between individual liberty and collective equality, it is the opinion of the majority of active political agents that decides the outcome. The struggle continues in all democracies of the world. But when the very definition of freedom is twisted to mean "freedom *from* want" devoid of all aspects of "freedom *to* be," then the once virtuous democratic struggle is merely a fraud. Liberty has already lost.

Socialism and the Chains of the Collective

Socialism's definition of freedom, pragmatically speaking, is: the submission of the individual to the omnipotent Guardians of the Social Welfare. Socialistic mechanisms, preoccupied with the regulation of society according to a single ideological standard, usually generate a single ideologue who eventually gains a monopoly on the processes of government by virtue of his "integrity" with regard to that standard. The will of this ideologue is then forced upon "the masses" ("the masses" being people too uncultured to recognize the severe measures of political tyranny required to establish their own well-being) during a prolonged, if not permanent, period of dictatorship - following the "scientific" Marxist adaptation (however paradoxical and absurd) that a stateless Utopia is best achieved by way of a supremely powerful state. The natural position of ordinary men in these collectivist systems is anonymous servitude to the needs of others within society, achieved through voluntary slavery to the state. The complex and often fragmented "General Will" described by democratic theory is diminished into the "Specific Will" of the socialized Collective. The Collective becomes a moral and political chain binding each person to the will of the government, which translates into the will of a single demagogue or a small group of party leaders. There exists no freedom outside the *duties* of the Collective, which are assigned, of course, by the wise (totalitarian) elite.

This interpretation of Freedom is utilized by military, civilian, and religious socialists alike, for it provides total power to rulers, no matter what their denomination.

In societies where the ethics of socialism are dominant, everything must support and contribute to that fantastical concept, the Collective.

THE NEW AGE POLITICS

In real terms, this means that very little is actually contributed. For example, consider the field of science. Knowledge acquisition in socialistic societies must be for the purpose of furthering the prescribed good of the Collective. But without knowledge acquisition being tied to individual fulfillment, little new knowledge is discovered. Invention and motivation are denied their true creative impetus: personal curiosity and satisfaction. In addition, any new knowledge discovered or created becomes the exclusive property of the Collective, just as the decision whether or not it will be utilized, and by whom, is up to the Collective. Economic as well as intellectual incentive is smothered. The spontaneous lines of communication-by-interest-and-talent are replaced by centralized directives and paranoid censorship. It is no wonder why socialism does not foster scientific advancement.

Furthermore, any pursuit of knowledge which might clash philosophically with the insulated beliefs of the Collective is barred or ignored. Consider the malevolent disregard of the brilliant work by Jewish scientists, and their eventual expulsion and extinction, by the Nazis in the thirties and forties; the Soviet rejection of genetic theory in the forties and fifties due to their rejection of evolution theories; and the continual censorship of artists and intellectuals who display unyielding individual inventiveness and espouse the dangerously unsocialistic concept of universal human dignity throughout the communist world.

Whether it be intellectual inquiry, industrial productivity, social justice, or ethical autonomy, the heavy chains of socialistic mechanisms grind all hope of progress to a halt.

Why, then, do most of the countries of the world, especially "under-developed" ones seeking dramatic economic growth, so quickly embrace socialism? Can they not recognize the chains of the Collective? Perhaps they long for a global socialism in which their own glaring need will give them a "right" to the fruits of wealth that seem to exist *a priori* in the free world. Then they won't have to create, but only take. Their economic growth can be both instantaneous and painless (and, oh, how their adoring citizenry will cheer them for their economic miracle-making).

To these people, freedom is a luxury of the wealthy. It is not viewed as a contributing element in the creation of wealth and growth. The right of individuals to possess property is merely a bourgeois rationalization, a rich man's contrivance which keeps wealth, land, and power in the hands of those who already possess it. The only realities are the needs of the masses. If coercion is what it takes to have those needs satisfied, so be it.

It seems to me, however, that this line of thought is overtly cynical and unethical. Most people, on the other hand, embrace socialism because they actually see it as a moral system. Socialism provides them with a utopian vision of unified peace, shared prosperity, political participation, and personal security, answering their most fervent wishes of an ethically ordered and contented world. And compared to the oppressive dictatorships most of them have had to survive, socialism seems to be, at the very least, the lesser of two evils. In a historical perspective, what might be termed "democratic socialism" is understood as a freeing force, a step toward a truly fulfilling self-sovereignty. It promises to remove the modern vexations of mechanistic alienation, chronic unemployment, slavish poverty, personal meaninglessness.

If these are the prevalent assumptions, then it is easy to see why socialism is the dominant political system in the modern world. Merely a pragmatic argument describing the benefits of the free market will not sway the opinion of those who believe socialism to be moral. They must come to understand that collectivism is not merely a chain on economic progress, but a chain on individual fulfillment.

Socialism denies human dignity; it does not protect it. It postpones human joy; it does not achieve it. It fills only the leaders' purses; it does not fill men's bellies or fulfill men's lives.

The word must be spread that for the greatest amount of people to benefit from prosperity, individuals must be free to work, profit, perform research, and live in a free environment protected *by* (and not *from*) individual rights; that a world of universal justice can only be founded on individual liberty; and that peace through voluntary cooperation and mutual benefit is the only true and lasting kind of peace.

THE NEW AGE POLITICS

Salvation Politics and the Yoke of Faith

Christianity's definition of freedom, what might be labelled "theological liberation," is the death of self to Christ. It is a kind of transformation, where the ego surrenders itself to the will of Christ and receives the gift of everlasting life in return. It is an individual act of faith; the supremely Christian act.

Salvation Politics adds to this dogma the assertion that through this graceful act, mankind is saved, not merely for the purpose of achieving spiritual immortality, but saved in the here and now, in flesh and spirit. He is not only made One with the Body of Christ, but given the gift of Divine Purpose as well. By living one's active faith, the Divine Plan for Human Salvation is to bear fruit *on earth*. In this manner, Christ is said to work *through* His Church, through history itself. Faith becomes a religiously social activity, one meant to purify not only the individual soul but society as a whole. Thus, what began as an extremely personal act is transformed into a supremely political act.

Before the cruel consequences of this assertion are discussed, it must be asked: what is the nature of faith, as it is devised by the advocates of Salvation Politics?

Salvation Faith is not a *love* of self and of one's values. It is not *charity* toward one's neighbor. It is not *loyalty* given out of earned respect. It is not *hope* in the future based on humanistic optimism. It is not rational *trust* gained from experience. It is not necessary *reliance* due to circumstances. It is not *theory* or *hypothesis*, not a rational projection of factual data through deductive analysis. Salvation Faith is differentiated from these other concepts because it is a belief in something *beyond* human sensory experience. Salvation Faith is an acceptance of that which is unprovable and has no basis in empirical reality.

This sort of unreasonable faith must be contrasted to the more reasonable kind that nourishes loving, caring people and augments their gratifying concern for their fellow man. One faith forces man to accept what would otherwise be absurd nonsense, while the other satisfies the soul with experiential testimony as to its legitimacy and worth. But unreasonable faith is demanded by practitioners of Salvation Politics at the exclusion of the more reasonable alternative precisely because of its irrational aspects: if unreasonable faith is the sole fount of Eternal

Salvation Politics and the Yoke of Faith

Truth, then common man will need professional assistance to understand what that Truth commands. This insidious hierarchy makes the common man into a mere tool, an empty vessel - a position he is supposed to exalt.

To a person who really wants to *control* his own destiny, unreasonable obedience is the last state desired. He does not wish to merely *guess* at what some religious dogma might expect of him or *accept* the professional revelations of the religious elite, but discover, through rational inquiry and self-responsible experience, what sort of life will be individually satisfying. To such a person, irrational faith is a yoke which delimits life, keeping him from implementing consistent rationality and individual autonomy, as well as riddling with guilt and repression the creatively spontaneous workings of his audacious imagination. Salvation Faith drives a wedge between the naturally effective processes of consciousness and the facts of reality, substituting knowledge with fiction, learning with revelation, ethical judgment with pious acceptance, and experience with restrictive moralizing.

But advocates of Salvation Politics do not desire free thinking individuals. Their only goal is a saved society ordered by the Sanctifying Virtues of their dogmatic fundamentalism.

The modern emphasis on reasoned skepticism has greatly diminished the harm wrought by strict adherence to unreasonable faith. Yet our culture still extols faith as a psychological ideal. In practice, such an ideal leaves nothing to fall back on but emotion.

Remember that faith, by definition, cannot be guided by reason, for it must *supersede* it. In matters of faith, a believer cannot depend on reason, he can only utilize reason as a tool to decipher the intuitions of faith. But what makes up these intuitions? In lieu of direct and personal revelation, there are only two choices: credulous dependence on outside authority or an unwise reliance on fuzzy emotionalism. Both are driven by an irresponsible and blinding desire to believe, an openness to either external or internal emotional manipulation.

The mechanism for transforming emotional religiosity into political monopoly predates written history. The modern practitioners of unreasonable faith fit in well with the ancient masters of mass emotion manipulation.

Of course, the spectacle of such emotional manipulation should not demean the humble, helping, humanitarian Christian communities of the modern faithful. Indeed, strict and unreasonable blind faith is attacked by mainstream Christians the world over as cultist and perverse. Reasonable faith, as an interactive human activity, is a source of great personal fulfillment and communal security. But the line between salvation theology and Salvation Politics is thinner than first suspected: it is a distinction of common sense rather than theological argument.

When confronted with the rantings of tyrants, wherein faith is merely a synonym for exploitation and deception, Christians rebel as true Knights of Humanity. When faced with extremists who desire to disrupt the social fabric through terrorism, to whom unreasonable faith has become the perfect opiate to induce violent martyrdom, Christians repel in horror and indignation. But when approached by those who desire, with infectious zeal and religious enthusiasm, a perfect society, faith can become a tool for social action that drowns any and all beneath its sweeping, sacred vision.

If the Divine Plan is manifested through the social works of faithful practitioners on earth, nearly any action, if done "faithfully," can be sanctified if it promotes the Great Religious Vision, no matter what the empirical or moral consequences. The social mandate of a "Just Order" becomes a political mandate for absolute authoritarianism. Big government becomes the single institution equal to the task at hand. Thus, Salvation Politics demands not just the faithful acquiescence of believers, but the sanctification of the State as the Right Hand of God.

There is only one system of social organization that can embrace the spirit and vision of Salvation Politics: world socialism. Why? Because socialism is not motivated by the "perverse and unchristian" self-interest of individuals as is capitalism. Rather, it is motivated by the sacred Good of the Collective. Socialism speaks to *society's* "holy" need, to an "aggregate happiness," not to the egoistical assertions of individual *self*-fulfillment. Complementing the fundamentalist's virtue of unreasonable faith, socialism demands that each citizen bend his will to the leveling demands of an egalitarian God, or, if one rejects the concept of a Spiritual Almighty, to the will of the modern deity called History. The entire globe must be purged with the vengeance of God, or the Great Dialectic, so that temptation and individual vision will be everywhere snuffed. Only socialism will enable rulers to possess the complete and centralized power they need in order to make sure people "do good." After all, don't holy ends justify worldly means?

To underscore this point, consider the social agenda of the American Catholic Bishops or the World Community of Churches. They speak eloquently about human dignity and the desire to liberate man from poverty, want, and degradation. Wonderful sentiments. But these practitioners of unreasonable faith not only disregard the obvious connections between the creation of wealth and individual liberty, they fail to recognize the equally obvious connection between human dignity and the need for autonomous self-responsibility. Like souls who need only to be passively filled with divine grace in order to be complete, they imagine human dignity as a hungry mouth needing only rice and grain in order to achieve fruition. Their single-minded demand for "compulsory charity" includes the forced redistribution of goods, the endless expansion of the Welfare State, the regulation (bordering on strangulation) of commerce and capital for "just" ends, the manipulation of the poor for political purposes, the dissolution of the family's and neighborhood's economic interdependences, the replacement of individual choice with moral authoritarianism. Human beings, as self-directed moral agents, count for naught; in the short term, only the number of full bellies matters - in the long term, only the advancement of the Saving Vision endures.

Salvation Politics suffers from its own suicidal renunciation of rationality. It fails to recognize that **one cannot alleviate poverty without knowing what it takes to create wealth. One cannot diminish want without knowing what it takes to achieve self-fulfillment. One cannot get rid of degradation without consistently upholding individual dignity.**

The mere *desire* for a thing is not enough. Every ethical person would like to see poverty alleviated. But what kind of person stops at the desire and goes no further? Perhaps someone who believes prayer is sufficient in attaining desires, someone whose faith "can move mountains." Perhaps someone who believes like a child that desires should be fulfilled merely by the *desiring*, and not by the *doing*; someone who disconnects or does not bother to connect actions and consequences; *someone who does not employ honest-to-goodness reason.*

And so the humble belief in Christian love is twisted into a demand for political oppression. The peace of spiritual virtue is distorted into a mandate for intolerant authoritarianism. A respect for individual human life becomes a call for parasitical altruism. The believer, challenged by church authorities on every side, falls back on his salvation theology for support. But his concept of freedom has already been turned inside out, reassigned as beatific servitude and self-sacrifice. He is paralyzed by the contradiction that makes his "liberation" synonymous with a "death of self."

Martin Luther had a much more consistent answer to the problem of freedom within the context of Christian theology:

> If we believe it to be true that God foreknows and foreordains all things; that He cannot be deceived or obstructed in His foreknowledge and predestination; and that nothing happens but at his will (which reason itself is compelled to grant), then on reason's own testimony, there can be no free will in man. (*Bondage of the Will*)

Instead of disciplining the self with reason and self-responsibility, Salvation Politics seeks to dissolve an otherwise unpredictable and often times destructive free will by replacing it with pious deferment to a Greater Will. It reserves for itself, however, the exact enunciation of that Will.

Moving beyond the democratic "General Will," past the socialistic "Specific Will," we now arrive at a comprehensive "Only Will." Man the Creator becomes man the Beast of Burden, accepting his duty with the placid acquiescence of an ox, numbed by the constant propaganda that declares escape as not only vain and presumptuous, but satanic as well.

At root, the fallacy of Salvation Politics is that in the world of politics, salvation is impossible. Although injustice must be minimized, in the arena of human interaction there will never be a time when men are able to live without conflicting with each other, without misunderstanding each other, without exploiting frequent opportunities to manipulate each other. And, most importantly, there will never be a time when men will be able to live without the responsibility of choice, beyond the consequences of their own frailties and failures. The tragedy is that, despite pronouncements and prayers to the contrary, authoritarian government is, more than any other institution, an instrument of conflict, misunderstanding, manipulation, and, above all, irresponsibility, all the while perpetuating itself by a false hope, a mistaken vision, a fatal faith.

Humanism and a Unified World Order

The modern humanist movement, claiming roots from Socrates to Jefferson, found its modern voice as a reaction to fascist repression, especially with regard to the unification and expansion of Germany. Its original goals were the protection of intellectual freedom (free thought) and the pursuit of world peace, yet its political program was heavily socialistic. Since the appearance of the Humanist Manifesto I (1933), the movement has been colored by Marxist language and ideology. It was believed that in the pursuit of both intellectual freedom and world peace, the best chance for humanity rested in the establishment of a single World Federal Government. Only such an all-encompassing body could withstand the challenges of the likes of a unified Germany, an imperialist Russia, an insolently independent USA.

In 1973, a Humanist Manifesto II was published, and its wording was far more liberal than socialist, but the socio-political mechanism for arriving at most of the described goals was still a Transnational World Government. The tendency to entrust or oblige to the state apparatus all manner of utopia-seeking power remained strong.

Humanism is, fundamentally, a moral revolution, a rebellion on behalf of rational human integrity. As a moral statement, I have very few points of disagreement with it, especially the libertarian humanism delineated in Paul Kurtz's *In Defense of Secular Humanism* (Prometheus Books, Buffalo NY, 1983). But the humanist vision of a Unified World Order is dramatically inconsistent with the basic libertarian tenet of universal self-sovereignty and must be severely criticized.

Imagine, if you will, what sort of political bargain would have to be struck by the liberal west with the communist east in order to balance the power of each respective state within any Transnational World Government. Keep in mind that the vast majority of the world's national governments, both east and west, are ardently socialistic. If the tally were by numbers only, liberalism would surely lose. It is clear that such a bargain would combine those aspects of government that *restrict* human behavior for the "benefit" of "the World."

How would such a bargain benefit the citizens of the world? It would not, for it would be designed by politicians to benefit politicians. Even the supposedly liberalizing forces of public pressure would assist this corruption, for a bargain would be mandated merely to reach a bargain at any cost - in order to placate the illusion-driven popular opinion of the democracies that movement toward unified peace had begun.

In short, we must not delude ourselves into thinking that any World Order would be as or more free than our own federally centralized system. To act on such a delusion would bring the most intransigent empire into existence that mankind has ever endured.

Could such a transnational concept ever be feasible? Why would a relatively free population of people wish to become subjects of a world - wide regime that promised an increase of political oppression? It would be like citizens of the United States demanding to replace their own Congress with the "Third World"-dominated United Nations General Assembly. Hardly a feasible consideration.

Perhaps their motivation would be humanitarian. If the people of the U.S. gave up a few of their liberties in order to join a World Order, people of, say, Vietnam, might be able to enjoy more liberties than they do now. The end result, on a world-wide scale, might be in favor of increased sovereignty for the majority. World Democracy would, for the first time, be a reality. Human perfection certainly would not be far off.

Perhaps their motivation would be guilt. Bowing to the envy of the world's poor, they might consider turning over all their property rights to those "more in need." The starving masses of India could set industrial regulations and world taxation policies. Perfect social justice would certainly have arrived.

Perhaps their motivation would be fear. If all governments were disarmed by a transnational super-super-power, the threat of war, especially nuclear disaster, would be throttled once and for all. Indeed, this argument is used by pacifists the world over.

But such a vision is terribly naive. The present world scenario might be pictured thus: six continents, enumerable islands, and vast tracts of water all partitioned, in a rather unsettled and anarchial fashion, by several gunslingers of various sizes and levels of egocentric idiocy.

Humanism and a Unified World Order

(One continent is too cold for human habitation, so it is regulated by a committee representing the more powerful of the above gunslingers.) All of these gunslingers claim a monopoly on organizational authority, political justice, and paternalism within (and many times beyond) their (often disputed) boundaries. If these independent gunslingers were disarmed by a single Almighty Sheriff, armed with a combined US-Soviet-French-British-Chinese-etc-etc stockpile of nuclear weapons, it is highly unlikely that peace would result. In fact, the chances of these weapons being used would increase, not decrease. Why? Just as bullets and bombs are used to subdue a recalcitrant or rebellious citizenry the world over, every large scale effort at dissent or liberation would be met with the threat of nuclear retribution. The mechanism for obtaining a moral/political go-ahead for using nuclear weapons would be all the more stream-lined and marketable. And no entity such as NATO or the Warsaw Pact alliance would exist as a counterbalance. Far from outlawing the possession, use, or production of nuclear weapons, such a Sheriff would find it prudent, if not necessary, to simply outlaw everyone *else's* possession, use, and production.

(Recall that the only nation to have used nuclear weapons was the predominantly Christian Democratic United States, and they not only dropped one, as a threat of more to come, but a second as well. The single reason they used such devastating power was that Japan could not retaliate in kind.)

Intranational politics is spoken down the barrel of a gun. The same would be true of transnational politics. But international politics is a game of "tit for tat," which, for forty years, has kept nuclear explosions confined to relatively isolated test sites. This may leave us with the insanity of Mutually Assured Destruction. But a utopian Transnational Order would have no checks or balances whatever and is the greater of two evils. A Utopian World Sheriff might free mankind from war (although even that proposition is rather farfetched), but it would replace the present scenario with a higher level of state-sponsored violence and coercion. Undoubtedly, the problems of crime, hunger, and productive meaning would be exacerbated as well.

It is inevitable that the governments of several nations would refuse to give up their localized power base, either to protect its citizen's sovereignty or its own. How would this obstacle be overcome? A World Order would not be possible unless the initial Transnational Congress declared war (through trade, extortion, or out-

THE NEW AGE POLITICS

and-out armed confrontation) on all steadfastly independent states. The peaceful humanist vision would deteriorate into one compelled to aggression.

Indeed, it will never be in the self-interest of governments to disband and join in a Transnational Federal Democracy - except, perhaps, to watch the dissolution of its enemy governments (if they do likewise). The sole interest they might entertain is in expanding their present power base (as was done at Yalta between FDR and Stalin). But the end result would be heightened divisiveness, not World Unification. Only complete conquest can create unification.

A political World Order may be more a symbolic vision than a realistic goal. Feelings of brotherhood and benevolence are worthy of propagation, but political unification is not the same as peaceful coexistence.

The desire for human happiness is a major impetus within humanism, but the pursuit of that desire on a political level must be placed in the context of individual sovereignty and unyielding human dignity, else the only choices open to man will be the distopian visions of Huxley's socially engineered passivity or Orwell's confrontational paternalism. Both visions grow more monstrous the broader their boarders become; the existence of a World Order would make a Brave New World or a 1984 far more simpler to achieve.

In the end, we must ask ourselves: What is it we actually want to achieve? We must be ever mindful of consequences. After all, from the consequences of our present decisions come the lasting legacies of the future. If we desire a world in which human dignity is nourished in a free and supportive community, making people equally oppressed beneath a centralized global authority is hardly the answer. Indeed, personal freedom may have a better chance of expanding within national borders, as every nation competes for membership and profit in an increasingly libertarian global economy. The humanitarian goal of true personal sovereignty might then be achievable, without the addition of another parasitical layer of governmental authority.

True freedom entails *no* sacrifice of one's mind or life to anyone. That is what being free means: "able to choose for oneself." A respectful harmony between free people is a highly ethical goal; but coercive unification, whether it be an assertion of the General Will, an expression of the Collective, a prescribed standard espoused by one of the world's popular religions, or a humanistic symbol of worldwide brotherhood, cannot lead us there.

LIFE, LIBERTY, AND THE PURSUIT CALLED HUMAN DIGNITY

Enough of criticism. After briefly sorting out some of the more prominent and destructive distortions of freedom in the modern world, it has become painfully clear that what is lacking in all the above political attitudes is a proper context. A thorough and consistent ethical context which is able to both promote and delimit an effective Politics of Rights is desperately needed.

I realize that it is common in the liberal democracies to espouse an amoral socio-political context. Western man wants "objective" lawmakers who do not bring their own narrow values into their legislation. After all, who would want some demagogue to codify his twisted morality into laws we must all follow? Ah, but isn't that what politics is? The single demagogue is called a dictatorship. Majority-demagoguery is called democracy. Interest-group demagogues pitted against one another in checks and balances, each with "equal" representation, is called republican government.

If individual liberty does not happen to be the political goal held by the designated rulers, then even such a balanced and "constitutionally guaranteed" experiment as our own political system fails. Government becomes a master, no longer a servant (as the original design suggested). The reason: design is only the second stage. Ethical reasoning and opinion is the initial factor in determining political power and function.

I do not mean to imply that among these structures there are not superior forms of government relative to the others. Political mechanisms may well determine if true liberty can be protected. But it is the ethical opinions of the citizenry which determine the underlying social laws which permeate all political structures. It is the individual aspirations of those in power which determine the *use* of a particular structure. Political discussions cannot be held only on the level of structures. To miss this point is to misunderstand the role of governmental and nongovernmental social institutions which aid and/or impede so much of our life's actions.

The Relationship between Politics and Ethics

Political science is not merely a study of the philosophies and mechanisms of governments. Politics is a wider issue, pertaining to the organization of a society, the mechanisms (both public and private) for resolving conflicts between people within that society, and the relationship between individuals and institutions both inside and outside that society - whether these include governmental or nongovernmental activities. (After all, even anarchism is a political theory - which might be called a non-state socio-economic dynamic.)

Whereas ethics is a philosophy that identifies values and derives codes of action to achieve and sustain those values, politics is (or should be) a philosophy that identifies social structures and institutions which *protect* values, thereby promoting value-pursuit and value-maintenance. Political mechanisms do not create, but protect, and thereby promote, ethically conceived choices and actions.

Viewed in this way, politics becomes an outgrowth of ethics, with ethics setting the standards and objectives for political theory. The ends of human action - the purpose(s) for human living - are ethical considerations. The means to achieve those ends - the proper internal (psycho-physiological) and external (socio-political) conditions for ethical human action - are both suggested and delimited by ethical considerations.

It is not the task of politics to dictate ends or means. These things are dictated by ethical arguments. Political theory merely hunts for practical and suitable structures wherein those means and ends can be upheld.

Often stated goals of political theory miss the mark. Prosperity, stability, aggregate happiness, adherence to religious dogma - these things may have their selling features, but they do not promote ethical living in and of themselves. Prosperity can be won at the expense of justice when it is sanctioned for a privileged class, as in slavery, or if enforced through a more egalitarian model, such as when the prosperity of all citizens is leveled to compensate for (natural or unnatural) economic inequalities, creating a class of irresponsible parasites who survive off of the forced confiscation of the others. Progress, especially in the areas of personal sovereignty and individual dignity, is often crushed in the name of institutional or social stability. As for the myth of aggregate happiness, the nineteenth century maxim "the greatest happiness for the greatest number" has thrust upon modern civilization an immoral disregard and intolerance for minorities and granted to the power elite a righteousness unbecoming to the original precepts of republican pluralism. Lastly, adherence to religious dogma, in the eyes of specific believers, may promote "moral holiness," but for those who dissent, whether they be believers in a different spiritual code or a variant of rational humanism, such a socio-political goal is simply unacceptable.

When political action, by definition, is strictly separated from yet absolutely secondary to ethical concerns, its single task is that of value-protection (protecting values it cannot create but which it must recognize and insulate from third-party harm). But to remain a political apparatus for *all* citizens, only those individually conceived choices and actions which are consistent with the tenets of initial noncoercion can be universally upheld (else political action becomes, to some, a destroyer of values). Thus, a Politics of Rights is necessarily the only legitimately universal political philosophy.

Consider how ethical reasoning delimits political action: First, dignity is man's most fundamental and comprehensive ethical desire. Second, it is the single desire which extends to every human being a worthiness and respect. Third, this worthiness and respect requires each individual to be free from initial aggression. Fourth, the only political activity required from an ethical base of human dignity is the protection of a citizenry from initial aggression.

Consider how ethical reasoning suggests political mechanisms: First, the fundamental expression of human dignity is the *self-responsible pursuit* of personal happiness. Far from being a divisive activity of narcissistic pleasure, the self-responsible and self-expanding pursuit of personal happiness is, for each of us, a psychological affirmation of our worth as living beings. Second, such a pursuit requires a single social concept: universal self-sovereignty. Third, by embodying the ethical concept of self-sovereignty into the political one of self-ownership, a coherent political mechanism can be built. Through this mechanism, self-sovereignty can be protected, and thereby promoted, under the political concept of self-ownership. Fourth, from the concept of self-ownership, the entire array of individual rights can be derived and codified under a manageable category of "legitimate property rights."

It is not merely the freedom to vote for democratic leaders that we desire, but the ability to go our own way *regardless* of leaders (and their armies of followers). Social discipline should find its source in a reverence for other's rights (appropriately codified into law) and one's own ethical reasonings, not submission to arbitrary authority. Man wants an environment in which he can excel, pursue, be varied, and become integrated with his community along the lines of his own interests and affections. His dignity requires more than static happiness, but the freedom of pursuit. It is not merely to be happy, but to be self-determined. Indeed, self-fulfillment is a by-product of self-responsible pursuit.

It is not so much that man desires social security as he desires a socio-political environment in which he can aspire. A high degree of stability and security are elements which promote affective aspiration; however, it is not to state-sponsored dictates that he looks for the goals of his aspiration, but to himself.

It is *choice* which the Self-responsible Man wants secured. That is the essence of political freedom.

The Search for a Politics of Selfestness

All political philosophy is grounded in ethical predispositions. What are the ethical attitudes of modern politics? Are they able to support a Politics of Rights? Do they protect and promote human dignity?

The ethical philosophies that have most dominated recent political history can be generalized into three categories: selflessness, selfishness, and amoral determinism. To show why they must be abandoned, let us take a brief look at their political consequences.

(1) The Politics of Selflessness. The ethic of selflessness is the devotion of self to another, the subjugation of one will to another. It is the central social ethic of both Classical Christianity and Marxism.

But the politics of selflessness requires that the state itself legitimizes all moral activity. The state defines what and whose needs should be met. The state decides how best to meet those needs. The state, in effect, becomes "the other" in need, the medium through which everyone achieves moral agency. Consequently, moral action is that which the state demands, exclusive of voluntary initiative. Moral action becomes impossible without state sanction. The politics of selflessness requires the political centralization of morality.

The state courageously accepts the task of defining rightness or wrongness. There has never been one that refused. The exact definition is usually relative to the specific objectives of an elite (a specific religious sect, a ruling party's platform, guilty liberal millionaires, etc.), a struggling class (the poor, the proletariat, bureaucratic corporations, etc.) or as a collectivization of needs in terms of society as a whole. In practice, however, rightness or wrongness is simply that which the state ultimately proclaims, regardless of moral propaganda (and often in contradiction to previous proclamations).

When the ethic of selflessness becomes embodied in political mechanisms, the individual is no longer the essential consideration of law. Justice is defined in terms of collective value; individuals become means to an aggregate end. "Individual rights" suddenly becomes a contradiction in terms. Any form of regulation, reorganization, or social manipulation is justified if it serves other-than-self state-defined goals. In fact, coercive tactics are often preferred, even by an intelligent electorate. A moral and dedicated public, imbued with a selfless ethic, naturally advocates violent and centralized social manipulation because it demonstrates the ultimate inferiority of the individual to the collective power. Centralized action also appears to them the most efficient and scientific method for achieving moral ends. If the coerced individual protests, he is simply labeled an immoral outlaw and punished further for his antisocial attitude.

It is easy to see that selflessness does not give rise to or support individual liberty. On the contrary, it righteously stands as an enemy of not only liberty, but the very legitimacy of individual moral agency as well.

(2) The Politics of Selfishness reacts to this sort of social parasitism by denying the validity of all charity and benevolence, ushering in a "me against them" brand of isolationist individualism that inhibits human caring and self-expanding compassion. Morality is defined in strict selfish-interest terms. Any reverence for the general

social welfare, or even the specific welfare of loved ones, is viewed as a sign of moral weakness.

The concept of individual rights is upheld (on the surface, at least) within the politics of selfishness, but any attempt to expand these rights into the social arena (regarding ecological concerns, wide spread diseases and immunization, the issues of political and economic participation, involuntary unemployment, and extreme poverty, to name a few) is thwarted or ignored. If the problem cannot be solved through a laissez faire balance of selfish interests, then let us all be damned together, or, better yet, each man for himself to the bitter end.

The politics of selfishness is often espoused by anarcho-capitalists, but its practical applications have been exploited most frequently by a political and economic elite who distorts the ethics of true liberty into the mechanisms of privilege: corporate statists and the idle rich who wish only to consolidate their own power and wealth. If human need or frailty is exploited by overt socialist interventionism, they are quick to defend the individual; but if the same degradation occurs in the "natural" functioning of corporate capitalism, they fall back on legalistic language which swallows up individual dignity like a starving beast. What a man can't pay for, he simply does not deserve (including justice). It is as if the willy-nilly pursuit of prosperity acquires rights unto itself, dismissing the individual as ultimately inconsequential.

Within the socio-politics of selfishness is a standard of morality based on economic success. The dollar becomes a deity. Moral worth, instead of being an expression of individual importance generated through self-fulfilling action, depends solely upon one's monetary net worth. The poor, according to such an attitude, are a rather immoral lot, undeserving of aid or assistance. If the unemployed or working lower-middle class protest at this rich man's chauvinism, it is simply a demonstration of their tendency to desire what they don't deserve (such as equal rights under the law).

Selfishness cannot give rise to a true Politics of Rights, as it often promises, because it has no positive social element. It defends freedom yet ignores the issues of how one establishes the power of choice. It condones libertine license yet fails to uphold mutual respect. It supports free trade yet fails to protect the individual from the privilege of the rich. It espouses property rights yet ignores those with little or no property, basing justice on the dollar alone. It advocates entrepreneurship yet does not disdain monopoly powers. Individual liberty, properly understood as a right based on the ethical foundation of self-sovereignty, degenerates into freedom for freedom's sake. In the end, the politics of selfishness fails to uphold individual moral agency by refusing to protect human dignity from the aristocracy of entrenched greed.

(3) Politics Beyond Ethics. The French philosopher Jean-Paul Sartre stated that any systematic ethics is in fact impossible until society itself is more conducive to the maturation of the free individual, since the individual's practical ability to choose is, in fact, bound to the prevalent social organization. Determinists, on the other hand, deny the existence of morality altogether, since they deny man's ability to obtain objective knowledge, the possibility of self-derived purposefulness, and the existence of choice. The individual gains worth exclusively through social utility. All human activity is to shape man into that utilitarian mold.

Both attitudes suggest that it is the state's task to engineer this transformation. Man must be made into *something*, since he is unable to make himself. This implies the contradiction that those in power know what man ought to be made into and how to engineer such a feat, even though the leaders are presumably human themselves. But such illogic is beside the point. Man, first and foremost, is a lump of clay just waiting to be animated with social usefulness through governmental mechanisms. Ethics, and individual moral agency, are left in the dust. Only pliable utility remains. Man becomes a mere cog living for the sake of the socio-political engine.

Such a view of man animates the amoral materialism of communist regimes the world over. It has also seeped into the back rooms of democratic planners who desperately jockey for positions in the national scramble for power. It has even begun to enter into conservative rhetoric which places a premium on efficiency without regard for proper procedure. The mechanized view of man has great appeal for those who consider themselves qualified to play God, who worship order above all else, or who simply cannot imagine that individual men and women might be able to decide for themselves how best to live.

Social engineering is basic to the modern belief that scientific-political activity can create Utopian Man. But it is difficult to create human dignity when the existence of moral worth is denied outright. Politics beyond ethics demonstrates better than any other example the proposition that freedom must be ethically centered in self-responsibility. To deny self-responsibility is to loose through default all human individuality to the political mechanism of deterministic coercion.

(4) The Need for a New Ethic. Because a truly sovereign-minded individual cannot pursue comprehensive self-worthiness within any of the three systems just described, new ethics must be sought.

When free men enter what they believe to be a free world, they encounter commandments, coercion, and manipulation; a ghost town filled with hollow tradition, a strident status quo, and fear of change; a world in which people call the deep void within themselves souls, the limp grey organ between their ears a mind, the will of others purpose, the envy of others law, and the inner strength of self vice.

But human dignity is lost in any system which requires the mind, the essence of self, to be subjected to abuse, denial, repression, or outright destruction. Ethics should enable the individual to do more than merely survive or attain relative utilitarian status.

Ethical living should be a celebration of life, a heroic adventure of human triumph. Is it triumph over self? Triumph over nature? Triumph over others? Surely not. It is triumph *of*, not over, self. Triumph *within*, not over, nature. And as for others, there could be no ethical triumph *over* another human being. If each man is understood as being distinct and as the only *owner* of his own life, then such a concept of triumph is ethically invalid. Nor can there be a parasitical type of joy which is stolen from one for the use of another. There may be shared admiration, inspired actions by another's triumph, strengthened and expanded convictions in one's own possibilities in the light of another's success and creation. But the triumph of self is itself distinct and cannot be shared directly. Integrity has no external standards. Joy has no exclusively external source.

What must be found is an ethic which meets the human potential for joyful integrity.

(5) Selfestness as a Comprehensive Ethical Concept. An attempt is often made to designate such an ethic with terms like "enlightened egoism" or "libertarian humanism." I prefer to use my

own term, "selfestness." Selfestness better describes the goal of the human pursuit called individual dignity. It directly confronts, and rejects, the common choice that pits self*ish*ness against self*less*ness - an argument which ignores the joys of self-fulfillment and the depth of meaning human life can achieve. It declares the preciousness of a sovereign self without declaring war on self-expanding and compassionate involvement. It involves man's rational capacity as well as those desires which arise from reasonable faith and emotional satisfaction. It rings with the glory of man's cooperative pursuits as well as the quiet peace of individual contentment. It refuses to reject either man's self-responsible or social nature. Selfestness is aspiration without violence.

Self*ish*ness walls the individual in a narcissistic citadel of belligerence and excess. Self*less*ness alienates the individual from him*self* by denying the worthiness of internal esteem, autonomous need, and self-joy. But self*est*ness rightly equates the good life with the pleasures of a consummate, involved self. Unlike the old divisive moralisms, it integrates the heroic pursuit of an ever-widening potential with an accepting satisfaction of being oneself, healthy self-pride with healthy love (in the knowledge that love is an outward expansion of internal personal meaning, an inspired embrace of cherished values), and self-reliance with an acknowledgement of all the joys and needs gleaned from human association. Selfestness is the only ethical concept comprehensive enough to recognize the wide range of desires and motivations man requires for actual fulfillment.

In short, true *human* living is selfest life-making; not selfish other-exploitation or selfless self-negation. A truly human ethics does *not* dissolve, transcend, or enclose the self; rather, it points the way toward ever-expanding self-worthiness: self*est*ness.

(6) The Three Pillars of the New Age Politics. America possesses an ethical-political document which embodies the true message of selfestness, what might be termed the Free World's New Testament: the Declaration of Independence. Understood in it are these ethical conclusions: that the pursuit of selfestness is the foundation for life-making; that this must be done in a context of individual liberty; that the individual must be the basic and sovereign political entity; and that every person has the right to dissolve associations, political or otherwise, which harm their rationally derived and socially noncoercive ends. The Declaration of Independence asserts

that the only sovereign is the everyman - not an oracle, not a god-king, not a brute-king, not a ruling class, not an oligarchy, not a popularly elected demagogue, not a majority. Each man has a protected sphere of personal action and private property which is inviolate. The authors of these documents understood that no ruler could ever be so morally superior or even so knowledgeable that he might know better what ends individuals should live for. Life's ends are purely individual concerns. Politics is meant to protect a social context wherein the personal ethics of selfestness might flourish.

"Life, Liberty, and the pursuit of Happiness" - the basic rights of man. Every individual has a right to live his own life, to be self-responsible. This right requires that he be free to choose, free to act, free to rebel, free to create his own living meaning. The personification of this creative action is termed "the pursuit of Happiness." Within these rights man's dignity is implicitly acknowledged, inalienably protected, and universally promoted.

It is the task of the Politics of Rights to answer, or at least to continue to try to answer, this most moral of all mandates.

Part Two:

SOVEREIGNTY AND ASSOCIATION

Part Two:
SOVEREIGNTY AND ASSOCIATION

It is a common belief that for an individual to join into a beneficial association with others, he must sacrifice a certain portion of his personal sovereignty. This rule of thumb is nowhere more apparent than in democratic congresses which pass legislation no one likes, each member having had to compromise on every issue, yet which produces laws everyone praises as works of "great consequence."

Modern society is suffocating from the comprehensive quality of these great consequences.

A complementary belief is that without the subduing effect of centralized governments, men would tear each other to ribbons in selfish pursuits of separate and sovereign goals. Without governments, pastoral rural areas would be ravaged by innumerable Hatfields and McCoys and every metropolitan area would degenerate into the violently chaotic Chicago portrayed in 1940s gangster movies.

Governments everywhere are protecting citizens from these potential scourges with repressive weaponry Al Capone could only dream about.

If personal sovereignty is a human value, due to the undeniable relationship between freedom and fulfillment, then it would seem that every effort should be made to retain personal sovereignty within associations of every kind. Social rights must be outgrowths of individual pursuits of well-being, not predatory powers imposed on a citizenry by its ruling elite (whether that elite be a dictator or a democratic congress). In upholding universal human dignity, there are certain social rights individuals *must* retain in every association, rights which *neither* individual nor state action can limit or impede.

It is the task of Part Two: SOVEREIGNTY AND ASSOCIATION to make coherent the ethical-social foundation for those rights.

In so doing, it must be understood that an ideal association of persons is one in which each individual benefits, in which no one need sacrifice life-making values or selfest choice, in which trades are offered and compulsion is denied. Whether that association is a marriage, a neighborhood coalition, a corporation, a contracted business deal, or governmental action, the ethics of selfestness demands self-responsible sovereignty for individual members at all times.

Personal sovereignty cannot be weighed against the benefits of association, however. **Sovereignty itself is the fundamental goal and consideration in all forms of ethical associations.** Sovereignty and association are complementary concepts, forming the basis for ethical social motivation and action, and dictating the structure and agenda for ethical political theory.

SOVEREIGNTY AND ASSOCIATION contains the following sections:

    Voluntary Association
        A "Sovereign Self" Defined
        Sovereignty's Explicit Clarification: Self-ownership
        The Libertarian Extension: Recognition of Sovereignty in Others
        The Need to Belong
        Pluralistic Community

    Self-defense as Positive Force

    Justice
        Justice as Independent of God and Nature
        Justice as a Human Concept
        Justice as Independent of Social Evolution and Capitalism
        Law and the "Order of Consonance": Giving Justice Political Coherency and Stability

Voluntary Association

A "Sovereign Self" Defined

Personal sovereignty is a natural need that springs from man's psycho-physiology. It is the fundamental expression of the conscious mind, of man's internal capacity for and dependency upon intellectual autonomy, of man's freedom-as-personal-consciousness.

But personal sovereignty is not merely self-determination. A more accurate synonym might be **selfest-responsibility**, both intellectual and social. To do anything one wishes, such as drinking excessively, would not necessarily result in an outward extension of internal integrity and self-responsibility. The very real vices of sloth, wastefulness, greed, and the elevation of ignorance and superstition over wisdom and inquiry do not result in personal sovereignty, even though they might be self-willed. Because of this confusion, it is necessary to define what exactly is meant by a sovereign self.

As a tool of fulfillment, sovereignty's standard is self-responsibility in every aspect of thought and action. It calls for the courage to judge one's own life as well as one's connections to the lives of others within the context of life-making values. It refuses to sever these judgments from self-responsible action (and interaction). Thus, sovereignty is not merely self-determination, but inalienable moral agency, infinitely grounded in a vigilant and self-conscious **responsibility-in-choice**.

By viewing sovereignty in this manner, one is able to determine more clearly that the *social* aspect of freedom is secondary - a result of one's initial *inward* self-motivation. Freedom is both initially self-generated as well as pragmatically self-maintained and expanded. (It is *not* a species of state authority or economic prosperity.) Personal liberty is *in*dependence - dependence on one's inner being.

It is equally clear that sovereignty does not require the individual to transgress upon others or be transgressed upon - as is required by the principles of selfishness and selflessness. Sovereignty does not demand sacrifices from others or credulity of oneself. The sacredness of human dignity remains constant throughout.

Sovereignty's Explicit Clarification: Self-ownership

A socially explicit definition of personal sovereignty is embodied in the concept of **self-ownership**.

Self-ownership makes explicit the fact that the separate and individual entity that is you also *belongs* to you and is not anyone else's tool. It is a recognition that you are an end in yourself, that your life is *yours*. Self-ownership makes clear that you are *differentiated* from all other things by *being your own possession*.

On a psychological level, self-ownership promotes and protects the concept of self-worth, the central problem of human dignity. If you did not own your achievements you could not take credit for your accomplishments; self-pride could not be achieved. Likewise, owning your failures is the only way to amend what went wrong and make it right. It is the only way to retain internal integrity.

Self-ownership is the fundamental human right of each and every individual. All that is gained by way of self-esteem, self-identity, and honest insight can be destroyed if self-ownership is not employed daily. It must not be mutilated by family guilt, governmental decree, or religious dogma.

Also, **self-ownership is the fundamental social value** society *in general* should support. Nothing must diminish or destroy this value, or else the entire structure of a rational and cooperative society will collapse. Self-ownership stands as the single pedestal on which all peaceful and prosperous human intercourse rests.

The Libertarian Extension: Recognition of Sovereignty in Others

Specific self-ownership must recognize the general self-ownership of all other selves. Denying another human being self-ownership would deny that human being his right to personal sovereignty. Such a denial becomes an attack against the very existence of individual selves, oneself included.

What this means in a context of social interaction is that one person does not have the right to transgress against another's personal sovereignty. This translates into the immutable social ethic: voluntary association.

Voluntary association is personal association void of initial force or compulsion, void of fraud or misrepresentation, association based on a free exchange of values. The mechanisms of voluntary association are reasoned persuasion and trade with one's partner (as opposed to fear, envy, guilt, fraud, or compulsion). Thus, voluntary association recognizes and heightens personal dignity and creates the potential for the nourishing bonds of mutual value-attainment.

Such a principle of association is the only one which utilizes the peaceful (free from coercion) context of mutual respect. Since it can only be performed in a context of individual liberty, I have called it the **libertarian extension** of selfest life-making into the social realm. It is what is commonly referred to as the libertarian ethic: the refusal to utilize initial force in any human interaction.

This ethic is often discussed in terms of socio-economic theory. In the marketplace, voluntary association translates into "voluntary exchange" or "free trade." The ethical demand is that human dignity and personal sovereignty be the founding social values and self-ownership be the fundamental human right. Paternalism, in any comprehensive and long-range sense, and interventionism, in any nonecological sense, are strictly forbidden.

Note how voluntary association places a premium on self-responsibility. You must look out for yourself - not out of petty greed (desiring that which is undeserved); rather, out of the simple fact that in a voluntary exchange **values are defined by each parties' self-responsible desires and cannot be "equal" in any quantitative sense.** If a trade is free of force and misrepresentation, and both parties are healthy, free, and informed, then each has the individual responsibility to make sure the trade is beneficial to them*selves*. One party cannot dictate values for another in a free trade, since values are relative to the individual and each individual is recognized as sovereign. One merely makes sure they are getting a "good deal" by trading with regard to their *own* values. This is true fairness: a voluntary trade where no compulsion, intimidation, withholding of pertinent information, or fraud of any kind enters in -

and each side benefits according to the standards of their own well-being.

The same principle of fairness should exist within one's personal relationships. I mentioned voluntary exchange first only because within the marketplace relationships between traders are often better defined and the parties involved are better protected than in relationships between family and friends. This, however, is not so much a statement applauding the ethical state of world economics as it is a sad statement regarding personal relationships. Voluntary association is more often present, and relationships are often more "civil," in the impersonal marketplace than in turbulent personal relationships where fear, guilt, envy, dishonesty, and intimidation are commonplace. The coercive drama in a typical household is many times more devious and destructive than that played out between consenting adults within the realm of market profit-attainment.

Why is this? Perhaps people feel less confident about the direction of their personal lives and their ability to control them. Perhaps too many people confuse affection with leniency. Perhaps too many people confuse loving with submissiveness.

The fundamental problem stems from abdicating one's personal sovereignty. For example, it is clearly an abridgement of self-responsibility to blame your childhood circumstances, or the prejudices of your ex-spouse, or the demands of your boss, for actions you perform that are abusive to you or to others. It requires an abdication of self-responsibility to blind yourself to the fact that your actions in the present are being performed by *you* and to blame those actions on the distorted hand of characters in your past. In the final analysis, what is vital is not the circumstances of your childhood (or any other portion of your life), but your *reaction* to those circumstances. And, in the here and now, all reactions are actions which we have potential control over; they are not actions to which we are chained like pre-programmed automatons. It is our moral responsibility to remain aware of this fact.

Abuse is a crutch; whether it be an abuse of others or an abuse of self. It is a symptom of a deeper problem: loss of self-respect. It is an excuse for failure, for despair, for having no control over your own life. But such a crutch is turned into a cudgel that will crush all who use it or come to it for aid. It is a crutch which continues to weaken its wearer until he is completely disabled. When such a person asks, "You mean to tell me that I can actually cope without my crutch of guilt and fear and self-contempt?" my answer to him is, "I mean to tell you that **you are free.**"

Envy, guilt, prejudice, or loss of self-esteem too often lead to violent aggression, personal *and* political. Of course, adhering to voluntary association will not rid the earth of these problems, but it can limit the arenas in which they might find an outlet. The free marketplace, with its struggles for recognition and product rivalry, makes a positive arena in which envy can be transformed into productive competition and esteem pursued through productive efficiency. Also, there are noncompetitive associations, such as churches, which offer counseling, caring, and constructive inspiration, and present the possibility of healing our many wounds through human belonging and acceptance.

One cannot consider their friends or colleagues, brothers or sisters, husbands or wives, parents or children, as slaves; nor themselves as creatures of bondage. This is true in households as well as workplaces, in school rooms as well as churches, in union halls as well as seats of congress.

The champion of human dignity cannot limit his demand for freedom to the economic realm. Nor can he merely decry political coercion. Nor can he simply call for intellectual freedom and scientific inquiry. He must uphold the individual in every phase of living.

The Need to Belong

It is often stated, especially in "intellectual circles," that individualism is a cancer in the body of the global Human Collective. Self-reliance is not only a sham (since no one is totally reliant on themselves alone, but part of a complex web of interdependencies), it is anti-compassionate and unnaturally self-limiting. Individualism has the potential to tear apart the world through selfish disregard for others, through the pursuit of individual salvation at the expense of global survival.

This line of reasoning is fundamentally incorrect. The brotherhood of man is not something which must necessarily inhibit individualism; rather, it is a vehicle to fulfill the many constructive needs and urges of each individual human being. Compassion is not a species of collective pity; rather, it is a sensitivity and responsiveness to individual human need, pain, and frailty that is born out of an overriding sense of *self*-dignity (which, through constructive individualism, is understood as each person's rightful disposition). Personal sovereignty is at the heart of the human *need* for association; it is not a deterrent to fulfilling brotherhood.

It is not an embarrassment to our self-reliance to say, "We need other people." Needing human companionship is part of human nature. We need other people for many reasons. We need them in the daily quest for survival, within the economic structure of procuring (through trade or productive cooperation) food, shelter, and warmth. We need to have access to other intellectual insights for successful knowledge acquisition. We use their ethical judgments in honing our own convictions. We need other people for successful maturation, as inspiration, as mirrors to ourselves, as companions in value pursuit. We may even need people on the level of innate drives; something built into our physiology which satisfies urges on a nonconscious level. It is not paradoxical, but simply realistic, to recognize that self-reliance finds it foundation in supportive associations which help the individual pursue his selfest potential.

Neither is it an attack on individualism to admit, "It feels good to belong." It does. Working with others or sharing values with others greatly enhances the level of our own joy. We can extend the meaning of ourselves outward onto people whom we value. We can attain certain successes only when working *with* groups of people. Witnessing many people pursuing like values can bolster our own quest. They can help us keep ourselves going when alone we might have quit.

But what is needed is more than "close proximity" to a gathering of human beings. That is not brotherhood. We need quality relationships which fulfill our nature as sovereign individuals.

The joy of belonging is not found in being a nameless number in a nameless mass. Neither is it found in the groupings of people created through compulsion or some other arbitrary force. Voluntary associations grow from common pursuits of like values. We need to seek associations which help us *prosper* with respect to maturity, meaning extension, and satisfied living.

Belonging is not a blind need which enslaves our will to that of some group just for the sake of being a part of that group. We do not

THE NEW AGE POLITICS

need to augment our distinct viability or accumulate greater meaning by attaching ourselves to pursuits supposedly "greater than ourselves." We do not need to be a part of "a whole which is greater than its parts." We can find satisfaction without becoming a cog in some giant wheel of "universal significance" that would otherwise be lacking in our own solitary lives. To put it bluntly, it is not a human need to be exploited. Such a perversion of belonging is at the heart of self-sacrificial slogans which animate movements like Naziism, Leninism, and fundamentalist Islamic terrorism. They do not create associations of brotherhood, but compulsory brother-to-brother servitude. They fill one's true need for the healthy maturation of personal identity with a temporary and self-annihilating other-dependency. They are need-defeating, like eating sugar to fill a starving belly.

The German philosopher Hegel stated that individual fulfillment can only be achieved when the self is totally aligned with the State, when all desires are unified in the Will of the Nation. The Federal Government provides the only authentic apparatus for "self-actualization." But what does this really mean?

Marx sought the same group fulfillment through the Classless Society. The Will of the People must become one's own will. The Goals of the People must be one's own goals. The attainment of that Will and those Goals provide the only lasting human fulfillment. But what does this really mean?

Both the German State and Marxist Societies utilized a great deal of initial force to bend the People to their Will. Voluntary association was not only outlawed in these systems, but condemned as the most monstrous form of social interaction. The sovereign individual was outlawed because the group, or the Will, was the fundamental social unit. The sovereign individual was immoral, by definition, because "moral wholeness" was achieved only through the subjugation of individual will (that damnable ego) to the General Will (that bigger-than-life sanctifying force).

It is no surprise that force or fraud is required to make a sovereign people "belong" to something with which they do not agree. The Will of the State is nothing more than brute force directing people's lives according to the designs of tyrants and criminals. The socialists' Classless Society is nothing more than a fraud, a lie, a cover for the two-tiered social order: the elite rulers and the nameless ruled.

In reality, there is no such thing as General Will, only the specific wills of conscious individuals. There is no such thing as Society, only many citizens living in varying kinds of associations. There is no such thing as a unifying State or a single apparatus of National Fulfillment, only elite individuals with power to usurp the personal sovereignty of the citizens within their domain. Only the individual is part of flesh and blood reality. Everything else is an intellectual abstraction and a generality used to comprehend and analyze social behavior and define different social groupings (associations both voluntary and involuntary). These groupings should *not* be used as the basis for law or ethics, as collectives which inherently deserve special privileges, distinct rights, corruptive immunities, or the power of leadership.

The Hegelian and Marxian equations become: fulfillment is won only through the subjugation of you to me. But that is slavery, not fulfillment. One does not belong, one is imprisoned.

The problem is that individual integrity displayed by one person alone cannot create a consentaneous society. It requires many people to make ethical political theories part of an over-all social framework. But the individual, regardless of the numbers of sympathizers, must be his own moral agent. He must be the ultimate protector of his own life and values. His own life must be his source of strength. His own fulfillment must be his own source of joy.

> To give up your individuality is to annihilate yourself. Mental slavery is mental death, and every man who gives up his intellectual freedom is the living coffin of his dead soul.
>
> (Robert G. Ingersoll, 1833-99)

In the face of an ever-growing socialization of human living, what must be repeated again and again is that individual sovereignty and belonging are not conflicting concepts. True belonging is in fact an extension of the self - a recognition of the value other individuals embody within the context of selfest ideals and pursuits. Human life and human joy are possible only when man is free to be self-responsible within voluntary and supportive associations.

Freedom, in the most comprehensively human sense, finds its home in healthy, respectful, and voluntary communities, not in isolationist individual disassociation, not in impersonal institutional membership, and surely not in coercive and hierarchical involuntary orders. Within a voluntary, cooperative community free individuals maximize potential choice as they expand outward in meaningful participation and affection. In fact, personal cooperation and productive friendship are the hallmarks of a self-sovereign people. In the end, sovereignty *encourages* community, responsible cooperation, and the universality of human dignity.

What is in conflict is sovereignty and collectivism, need and self-sacrifice, belonging and subjugation.

Pluralistic Community

If community is central to the positive interaction between sovereignty and association, an attempt should be made to define it more precisely.

Cicero stated: "A people is a gathering of those united by agreement on the right and by shared interests."

But the belief that community centers around an agreement of what is right simply belies the facts. A pluralistic people, like our own, have many divergent views of "the right," some which are not only contradictory but mutually exclusive; yet Americans exist as a people. In fact, the genius of our conservative and decentralized socio-political apparatuses enables differing visions of "the right" to coexist in compromising harmony. Perfection of *any* specific "right" is beyond reach, much to the relief of those who view "the right" in differing terms. The glue which makes individuals "a people" is something more transcending.

Likewise, it is little more than a tautology to state that communities share common "interests." So do clubs, culture societies, any one of the many national and multinational corporations, any one of the 200 established religious denominations in America alone, etc. It may be that a specific American citizen shares more interests with a business partner half way around the globe than he does with his next door neighbor. A special kind of shared interest binds "a people," something beyond mere inclination or commercial need.

Although a people must agree on (or at least acquiesce to) the legal *processes* in which "wrong" action is judged (the mechanisms of due process, representative legislation, civilian policing, etc.), something more akin to *faith in consonant aspiration* and *common sympathy* unites them as a people: what might be termed "constitutional reverence." There is a transcending element of "the sacred" in community which combines individual people in sustained harmonious pursuits, and which, when missing, opens up a gathering of people to interest-group anarchy and divisive posturing in the name of disparate definitions of "the right." (See M. A. Kaplan's *On Freedom and Human Dignity*.)

This sacred aspect of community is often implicit in talk of a people's common *identity*. The problem with common identity is that it often turns into aggressive tribalism, righteous intolerance, or similar dispositions which attempt to purge a group of those who, regarding a closed and elitist definition, do not conform (such as Jews, atheists, immigrants, aborigines, millionaires, the homeless). A major aspect of "identity" is its ability to *dis*associate one gathering of people from another. It is mutually exclusive, not transcendentally binding. If consonance within pluralism is to be sustained, something other than "identity" is required.

Community, in fact, is extra-political. It has more to do with family than government, tradition than geography, love than law. The roles and goals of education, commerce, and custom are more influential and binding than that of legislator and magistrate. The reason is that community is not a monolith sculpted by leaders to which acquiescing followers happily prostrate themselves. Community evolves as a bond among striving individuals. The central identifying features of community come from visions of self-responsible security, personal well-being, and mutual progress, not mere law and order.

The sacred aspect of community must be understood in these terms. The bond that exists among a people has nothing to do with a specific dogma. It is not a form of religious piety. The sacredness of human community springs up from the personal aspirations of human betterment, selfest possibility, fulfilled well-being. The interplay between interpersonal dependencies and individual desires, communal involvement and personal joy, founds ones allegiance to "a people." It is movement *toward* a general betterment, toward an ever expanding and pluralistic self-worthiness, that sustains and binds a people.

When the simple declaration of "One Nation, with Liberty and Justice for All" is superceded by "One Nation under God," as was done in the Pledge of Allegiance under McCarthyism (signifying, not a return to supportive Christian community, but a recognition of an already growing and paranoid separatism), divisiveness results. Are good people who happen to be agnostics, such as Henry Ford, Thomas Edison, and Albert Einstein, necessarily stripped of their citizenship by such a test? What about Buddhists, pantheists, or complete atheists? Isn't the concept of community larger than pledges and codes?

Community cannot be cast around an absolute vision, a religious test, a utopian righteousness. A nation does not exist "under" anything; rather, it exists *among* and *toward*. When religion replaces secular *human* sacredness, when proclamations of prophets replace personal aspirations, when promises from the supernatural replace the needs of the here and now, a common gathering of men becomes an elitist-led march set to the drums of sacrificial single-mindedness. Humble reverence is drowned in pious judgment. Voluntary, self-expressive, benevolent bonds are replaced by authoritarian commandments.

If conservatives can be blamed for thinking, erroneously, that compulsory religious devotion can build community, believing, as they do, that nonrational conformity is the cornerstone of social order and moral expression, then the liberal must be charged with the equally erroneous opinion that community can be induced through federal compulsory service. Falling over themselves in an attempt to cash in on the "new patriotism," liberals have rekindled the call for a system of national service by our youth, on the order of an intranational Peace Corp, so that these youths might "return some of the advantages and investments they have received from society" (Sen. Gary Hart) and "foster a new spirit of citizenship and patriotism" (Gov. Charles Robb). It seems the recognition of mutual benefit a young person feels toward his community can only be experienced as some form of "debt" which must be repaid through compulsory social work - as opposed to adding to that benefit through productive labor or attaining a higher education so to become even more productive. Imagine how thankful our youth will feel if forced to postpone self-responsible labor and studies with a year or two of planting trees or "counseling" the poor. Yet, compulsory service of innocent citizens would not be instituted merely to instill proper social graces into an all too bourgeois "me-generation"; as Professor Charles Moskos of Northwestern University has said, "The real advantage of national service is not to the young. The fundamental benefit is to society itself in reinstating its sense of comity, community, and service that we all seem to have lost." Recall how those virtues were nurtured so dramatically by the national service program the Pentagon ran during the 1960's and 1970's.

Community must live *for* and *through* its members. If it does not, conformity and compulsion will not induce it. If it does, compulsory service or legislated conformity will only destroy it.

Community requires genuine mutual respect among its members. Respect is not a by-product of compulsion. Respect is essential in the maintenance of what is sacred among a people: common sympathy toward the individual yet socially consonant pursuits of self-worthiness. But it is also required in maintaining general order in the streets, fairness in the marketplace, and respect for the process of rights enforcement. A lack of mutual respect results in cynicism, apathy, aggression and a general clamoring for totalitarian restrictions in the name of self-defense. If community cannot rest on internal, voluntary, interdependent respect, it will fall to pieces.

Consider the problem of the black ghettoes. Before there was centrally imposed welfare, these communities had to rely on themselves. Their material wants were relatively immense, but family/neighborhood bonds and emotional interdependencies were strong. Economic necessity required families and friends to work together, to rally around each other. Community leaders were chosen from those who had been successful as merchants, skilled craftsmen, and preachers; economic necessity required neighborhoods to support and depend on those who owned local property or who locally produced goods. If an individual needed a loan or emergency charity, he would have to go to a leader of the black community; there was little choice in the matter. Yet this reinforced the interdependence of the community as a whole, nourishing the sacred self-supportive sense of commonality. The pervasive moral sense among black communities was linked to economically productive criteria, strengthening the notions of responsibility and self-betterment.

This spontaneous reinforcement was replaced by white-sponsored welfarism in the Sixties. (The disastrous results are well documented in

THE NEW AGE POLITICS

Charles Murray's *Losing Ground*.) Now, if help is needed, blacks go to white social workers who not only dole out nonvoluntary tax money, but a "healthy" dose of elitist moralisms. Resentment festers on both sides. The traditional leaders of the black community have become irrelevant. They are even scoffed at, by some, as stooges of the "white system," Uncle Tom's who are too old fashioned (of high integrity) for their own good. A new black leadership has arisen, one that is purely political in nature, designed only to lobby white politicians for more aid. Ties of interdependence have been removed from the community, replaced by poor blacks needing white handouts and white politicians needing black votes. Hardly the nourishing kind of interdependence which builds self-esteem and communal betterment.

Consider the problem of racism in a small community. When a large Laotian refugee family moves into an all-white neighborhood, they are usually more than a novelty. Those who understand the hardships this family has endured and the trials they must still overcome extend sympathy, praise, and a helping hand. Other neighbors wait, wondering how the presence of nonwhite immigrants will change things. If it becomes known that the Laotians are on welfare, those who would be inclined toward skepticism and intolerance come to the fore, becoming cynical and aggressive.

There is nothing most Americans despise more strongly than a free ride, whether it be given to a minority welfare recipient or a wealthy corporation. All manner of freeloading is generally viewed as disgraceful. When one's own money assists in this freeloading (tax dollars for public assistance programs), simple envy and resentment turn into outrage.

Would a well-groomed, self-supportive Laotian physician have provoked such outrage? It is doubtful. Neither would a family completely sponsored by a neighborhood church or private relief organization which utilized the active involvement of several volunteer neighbors cause a groundswell of racists reactions. Under these conditions, any civil and dignified minority family would, undoubtedly, become an integrated and mutually respected member of the neighborhood.

But the introduction of tax-supported freeloaders into a neighborhood severs the ties of mutual respect that necessarily make up a coherent community. The real villain may not be racism; rather, it may be public assistance programs which destroy initiative not just in the poor and displaced (50% of whom are unable to get off welfare roles in a ten year period), but destroy the initiatives and benevolent tendencies of a community to be open and supportive as well.

The common stake of our society is sovereign well-being. Communities exist to protect and support this common stake, and individuals find fulfillment involving themselves in supportive functions. Insofar as the government circumvents this personal involvement, replacing it with "forced charity" and formalized programs, they destroy the possibility of active harmony among a pluralistic people.

Modern immigrants have far different obstacles to overcome than our own ancestors had. Rural, impoverished, illiterate refugees from modern war and oppression no longer find open spaces on which to farm or homestead. They are rarely able to locate areas of similar old-world customs and languages in which to settle as did our ancestors. Towering cities stand like mountains, forbidding rather then welcoming. And we as modern democratic citizens generally leave any aid up to our government, forgetting, in our affluence and our spirit of modern welfarism, what it takes to overcome these obstacles - what it takes to make a healthy community.

Immigrants flee their homeland and come to America not in search of a free ride, but for a place in which they might carry on in self-responsible freedom. We as Americans should be grateful for the trust these immigrants have in our pluralistic and free nation. Outrage against them is completely misplaced. Our critical eyes should be directed instead toward the involuntary system of welfarism which displaces self-fulfilling personal involvement with a state-sponsored, tax-funded bureaucracy.

Supportive community is a fragile and dynamic consonance. We must understand its origins and intricacies if we wish to protect the sovereignty and well-being of individuals through voluntary commerce and just law. The point of liberty is to unfetter the power of men and women and children in a supportive world. All citizens must cherish this insight.

The "nation-as-community" plays a vital role regarding the local dynamic of supportive pluralism. Recall how Martin Luther King, Jr., was protected from local police by the United States Marshalls. The 1965 Voting Rights Act enabled southern blacks to vote at federally protected voting booths, bypassing local obstructionism. Anti-war protestors, dissenting feminists, and radical environmentalists are regularly extended equal rights and due process, preserving a general constitutional reverence in the face of harsh local reactionism. The dynamic evolution of pluralistic community is supported on a national level, avoiding local lynch mobs and violent vigilantes.

In addition, the nation-as-community enables an ardently individualistic people to bind together voluntarily for mutual security in a National Defense. Without such a community spirit, a sprawling and varied nation such as ours could never remain of a single mind against the international threats that plague contemporary existence. This nation-as-community also binds its people in ever-widening spheres of interest, economic and cultural interdependencies, and political cohesiveness, strengthening their collective self-reliance while broadening their outlook and vision in times of peace. On a practical level, it also limits, through the recognition of national boundaries, the social obligations and altruistic benevolence members extend in order to maintain a mutually constructive "will to worthiness," keeping a citizenry internally charitable while protecting them from exploitation from without.

Unlike most governments, American "Government" is not a single entity and cannot be brought under a single vision. Mayors battle Governors who battle Congresses who battle the President who battles the Supreme Court. There is pluralism, contradiction, and conflicting ideals at all levels. What binds them together is an extra-political reverence of our common stake, a sacred allegiance toward consentaneous self-worthiness. We must preserve both the counter - balancing national federalism and the conservative instincts of localities, binding them together with the constructive aspirations of striving individuals.

True community is a libertarian federation of sovereign individuals joined in sacred allegiance toward an aggregate self-worthiness. But the usage of "aggregate" is not connected in any way with overriding socialistic authoritarianism. Internal consonance is a matter of positive personal aspiration, mutually recognized preciousness, interdependent voluntary commerce, and a reverence for the common stake: sovereign well-being. If any one of these aspects of communal consonance is missing, community disintegrates into inorganic stratification, no longer able to be sustained as an active, dynamic force providing sacred nourishment and irreplaceable energy to its members.

Pluralistic Community

The modern world has suffered greatly from the one-dimensional utilitarian viewpoint which defines people as tiny atoms crashing about like so many billiard balls, bouncing off of one another but never really changing each others character or make-up. Both conservative and radical advocates of liberty often confuse self-responsible sovereignty with this kind of isolationist separatism. But human longing and human need are chemically interactive with human involvement, creating a joyfulness that revels in self-expansion, competitive production, and cooperative success. Voluntary association must end (or begin) in community, else it will whither into narcissistic anarchy, utilitarian withdrawal, or authoritarian cynicism.

SELF-DEFENSE AS POSITIVE FORCE

Counterbalancing the license of self-determination, within a free society, is the right of self-defense. But it is more than a negative check against accidental or intended abuse - it is a positive social activity protecting both personal sovereignty and the social ideal of voluntary association.

In a voluntary relationship, both parties: (1) must be free of coercion (physically, emotionally, psychologically) or the threat of coercion (intimidation, extortion); and (2) must not be kept from knowing the true nature of the relationship that is being entered (fraud, misrepresentation).

If these conditions are not met, the relationship is involuntary. Sovereignty is abridged. Values are betrayed or destroyed. At least one of the parties involved is abused.

If necessary, force can be used to break free from involuntary associations. **Force has only one ethical use: the protection of values. Such protection is called "self-defense."** The value of defending the self must not be underestimated. It is a very valuable tool, and, in varying degrees, one used daily. It not only protects and/or wins back life-making values. Exercising the defense of self stimulates internal integrity and clarifies the meaning and importance of one's life and loves.

The libertarian extension demands that the initial use of force be renounced. Does the act of self-defense compromise this position? Must freemen be extreme pacifists? No. But self-defense must not be flippant or excessive. The retaliatory force used to protect one's values must not exceed that which is necessary for protection. It must be a calculated force which does nothing more than break the shackles of involuntary association. It must not become an exploitive force of legalized slavery or an aggressive force of reverse compulsion in the name of revenge.

Acknowledging the necessity of self-defensive force does not open the door to all manner of coercion. The right to self-defense does not infringe on or delimit the universal human right to self-ownership. When force is used by the victim against a transgressor - force that does not exceed that which is perceived as necessary to defend the victim's values - it (1) does not, in fact, infringe on the transgressor's sovereignty; (2) does not require compensation; and (3) is an ethically justified use of force which aids the over-all establishment of selfest ethics.

(1) How could harming someone, even if that someone is a blatant criminal, not infringe on their personal sovereignty? Simply, a transgressor (someone who is usurping another's sovereignty and values) is not acting as a sovereign individual (in the self-responsible, autonomous sense), but as an aggressive parasite. During his act of initial violence, he is not exercising sovereignty; he is, in fact, destroying the concept of sovereignty by doing violence to both his own and another's right to self-responsible integrity. Although, as a conscious human being, he has the *capacity* for sovereignty, he is not implementing it. The exercise of his sovereignty is not impaired by using force to stop him from further transgression. Likewise, his *capacity* for sovereignty (the ability to utilize self-responsible personal liberty in the future) is not necessarily injured within the confines of effective defensive resistance (except in the case of killing or seriously maiming the transgressor in the course of necessary defensive resistance, which, as is seen below, may not support the potential sovereignty of the specific transgressor, but does support the *generalized* ideal of sovereignty and may be ethically justified).

(2) Since the transgressor has damaged the victim's values by his initiating assault, any values the transgressor may have lost by the victim's proper exercise of self-defensive force are viewed as part of the compensation *due the victim.* They are an ethically justifiable part of the *effort of value-maintenance* required by the victim as a consequence of the transgression. This includes the effort to elude any potential damage due to intimidation, threat, and extortion. It also includes force required in obtaining subsequent restitution.

Even if defensive force requires taking the transgressor's very life, this is still viewed as necessary compensation within the confines of asserting sovereignty and breaking free of coercion. The extremely violent transgressor has broken all negative obligations which are included in voluntary association. He has forced his "trade" upon his victim. In effect, he is saying, "Your life or my life." The victim is not actually engaged in a trade when exercising defensive force, but **his act of self-protection is ethically equal to whatever force is required to equalize the perceived forced offered by the**

transgressor. He is engaged in a trade-off equation. The transgressor sets the terms (violence to combat violence) by his initial action.

However, the interpretation of these terms (the amount of self-defensive force required to defend against the perceived transgression) is *solely* the prerogative of the victim. The amount and severity of self-defensive violence is conditional to the *perceived* threat.

> The victim should have the benefit of the doubt about the amount of force which was necessary to stop aggression. Necessary force is not determined by facts that are learned after a rights violation has taken place, but by what reasonably appeared necessary at the time. If someone is being threatened with what she believes to be a gun, she can shoot in self-defense, even though the gun later proves to be a toy. Criminals assume the risk of being misunderstood...
>
> The amount of force which can morally be used in self-defense. . .is justified by the [positive] right to prevent and correct the violation, *not* by the size of the violation. (Alan Burris, *A Liberty Primer*)

(3) Not only does proper self-defensive force fail to impede the transgressor's at-the-time sovereignty, which he has not exercised, it may even aid him in the future utilization of his sovereignty. Self-defense denies parasitism. It also imposes the necessity that others must create or trade for their own values, for they are not able to steal them. You must be sovereign, for no one else will let you be sovereign over them.

Selfest ethics delimits the prerogatives of the community by making all interactions strictly voluntary, defining cooperative value-pursuit as the only sanctioned community activity.

The protective mechanisms embodied in defensive force help secure a peaceful, trade-oriented, cooperative environment in which the prevalence of transgression is minimized and productive security happily maximized.

JUSTICE

The basic ethical forms of social interaction have been identified: voluntary association and self-defense. Now the more difficult issue of how these activities are to be protected - the mechanisms of justice - must be introduced.

It is obvious that actual justice is not merely that which is lawful. There can be, and are many, unjust laws. Governmental decrees do not create justice. Likewise, social customs are not always just. Both mechanisms have evolved for the purpose of retaining a status quo; they are not meant to specifically protect ethical interactions between sovereign people regardless of socio-political rank. It may be common practice to identify the administration of state laws and the consequences of social conformity as the only viable mechanisms of "justice," but this tendency often realizes unjust consequences. The time has come to acknowledge that the true foundation of justice cannot be found in institutional ethics or hierarchical custom.

Justice as Independent of God and Nature

Adding to the dilemma are theological usages of justice. Misperceptions arise when it is believed that justice is somehow built into the very fabric of the universe, either as the workings of Providence or some more natural design. But in the world of physical nature there are no "rights" or "wrongs," there are only consequences. Life *per se* is neither just nor unjust, it simply is. To believe otherwise leaves one open to unearned guilt, unnecessary anguish in the face of powers beyond one's control, and the immense burden of unanswerable whys.

Demanding that the world is just "by design" either sanctifies the status quo or the raging mob, while robbing the individual of both his inherent responsibility and personal viability as a distinct moral agent. Theological arguments are dangerous in that they provide both the power elite and the envious rabble with absolutist language, making them the voice and delegate of Destiny. Throughout history, the delegates of Destiny have inspired intolerant inquisitions, apocalyptic crusades, slavish colonialism, fanatical class conflicts, and bloody, collectivist revolutions. They have never served justice.

Justice is measured by man alone. It is the measure of his fallibilities and as well as his highest aspirations. Justice judges man's sullied consequences against an infinitely human ideal of self-responsible living.

Justice as a Human Concept

The problem of politics, and its final hope as well, is that justice is a purely human concern.

Justice is not a mystery which requires priests or politicians to delineate. It is not an encoded body of knowledge which only specialized students of law can decipher. It is a system whose standard is intimately human: the notion of what is right and what is not. The trick, regarding political philosophy, is in understanding that the necessary *universality of justice* delimits the scope of political action.

Political power, to remain a universal tool, can only be used for the single, noncoercive end of protecting personal sovereignty. Any other use makes it a tool of privilege and exploitation. The power behind law enforcement must insulate an individual so he can assume the positive aspects of sovereignty; it must not be used to shackle the individual to the coercive, manipulative demands of others. Justice is a tool of security, not creation. Individuals create, either by themselves or in cooperation with others. Justice provides a means to discipline that creativity (and destructive capacity) so that openness, honesty, and reciprocity is retained in all human interactions. Justice is not to set the goals or forcefully channel that creativity toward specific ends.

In practice, the concept of justice evolves with human ethics. It cannot remain tied to either ancient scriptures or constructionist interpretations of codified constitutions. Such a fetter would arrest moral reasoning in some past epoch, making justice unsuitable to contemporary thought. (Note that both the New Testament and the U.S. Constitution were created in an age when, for example, slavery was tolerated without condemnation, aristocratic privilege was accepted and commonplace, and women were viewed as subservient to men - all viewpoints which modern civilization has, hopefully, outgrown). The concept of justice is grounded in rational inquiry and the cooperative interests of the society in question. It is eternally dynamic. This insight underscores the need to argue political issues from an ethical base.

The goal of political mechanisms - social justice - is inherently a species of popular opinion and general moralisms. If opinion holds that the status quo is an expression of some Natural Order, than the poor, the oppressed, and the slavish citizenry have a natural or divine role to play *as* the poor and oppressed; justice will not come to their aid. Conversely, if opinion holds that justice is the egalitarian sameness of all men, then the rich are unjust merely for being rich and the poor are allotted "rights" of confiscation merely for being poor. For any reason, if a populace believes in such things as "natural leaders," if they believe that individuals cannot progress or create social harmony without coercive leadership, justice will be used to insulate and perpetuate a necessarily innocent Aristocracy and laws will concern themselves only with augmenting that Aristocracy's already pervasive control of society.

Justice in the New Age must break the binds of authoritarianism, not augment them. It must uphold individual rights, not stratified hierarchy or institutional power or administrative convenience or collectivistic populism. It must use personal sovereignty as its standard, not governmental decree or scriptural commandments or rich men's prosperity or poor men's envy. If political action is to retain any legitimacy, it is as a protectorate of personal sovereignty and nothing else.

Justice as Independent of Social Evolution and Capitalism

The clearsighted perception that justice is linked to the evolving concept of social ethics does not mean that the political extension of justice is meant to *serve* "social evolution" in any manner. This mistaken belief twists justice into an agent of such abusive notions as the "Law of the Jungle" or "Survival of the Fittest."

"The Jungle," in these scenarios, is an amoral environment in which the strongest are supposed to survive while the weak perish.

Such a "natural" system is supposed to purify the human species, continuing the evolutionary forces of natural selection. Many view the capitalist system as a jungle-like environment where dog eats dog and individuals rise or fall according to their "competitive instincts." The fittest are supposed to survive, besting the rest of the competition, becoming executive Tarzans who supply future generations with their superlative seed.

This "seed" is not really genetic - not in the literal sense. In the context of "the evolution of society," the victorious businessman-apes pass on their superior "seed" by way of political power. Because they are more fit to succeed, they are more fit to rule. And the form and direction of their rule is to continue their own success - at the expense of those "less fit."

This concept of justice is suppose to serve the collective human species (by purging it of its weaker members) through the subjugation of the weak by the strong. Never mind that what defines "weak" and "strong" is usually a matter of race or nationality or class distinction or some other accident of birth. Social evolution implies that there must exist a natural genetic hierarchy to human associations and to the subsequent administration of law. This stratified hierarchy determines who rules and who obeys, who lives and who dies. The individual is of no importance; only the collective attributes of race or wealth or creed matter.

This attitude of Natural Hierarchy can be found today among people who believe, erroneously, that capitalism produces a spontaneous brand of natural justice. They exalt capitalism as a system which extols upon the honest, hard working entrepreneur success directly related to the effort and efficiency put out. Thus, the virtuous among us can be identified by the amount of their economic success. If this attitude is combined with the belief that the virtuous have a natural right to govern, the result is a pro-corporate "marriage" of capitalism and statism which puts into the hands of the rich even greater reigns of power. Instead of letting decisions up to individuals, corporate-statism presumes to set the goals for society (in much the same way mercantile aristocracies did in the Old World).

But capitalism does not necessarily identify the virtuous. Regardless of whatever benefits capitalism provides generally to a society, it is not, in specific instances, an actual Meritocracy. It is merely a tool of exchange. Riches are not bestowed upon the best, the brightest, and the most energetic. Riches are more often part of a family legacy or acquired through a complex mixture of cooperative associations, tangential enterprises, timing and location which spur on one's own good fortune in a generalized coattail effect. For every hardworking millionaire there are thousands of hardworking men and women of the middle class who find it increasingly difficult to pay their excessive taxes while trying to save for their first home, their children's education, or their old age. There is no question that individual initiative is needed to take advantage of fortune when it presents itself, or even to make ends meet on a daily scale. But individual initiative, in the final analysis, is perhaps more essential to individual fulfillment than substantial economic success.

In addition, what succeeds in a capitalist market is not necessarily endowed with virtue. Profit does not equate with goodness or well-being or even sovereignty. "Market value" tells us only where demand and supply intersect, not whether the demand or supply is rational, right, good, or ethical. Violence and pornography, especially when combined, sell very well as entertainment. Drugs of the worst and most debilitating kind bring in the greatest profits. All manner of superfluous products flood the market every day, accompanied by a deluge of insulting advertisements. Meanwhile, companies which provide services basic to human living often fail from a combination of bad marketing and lack of sufficient interest. The establishment of a free market, even if those who succeeded in it were kept from turning their wealth into political power, would not automatically create a virtuous world. Freedom is the *starting point* of virtuous human living; it can never be more.

However, the requirements of a capitalistic market include a respect for property, labor, innovation, cooperative initiative, forthrightness, and reliability. Capitalistic interactions depend on contract law, the protection of rights, and the outlawing of all transgressions. These are all healthy consequences. But their cause is not capitalism *per se*. Rather, it is the many demands of ethical sovereignty, the energy of individual aspiration and the pursuit of dignity, which has established the rules of free and harmonious commerce. It is not economic success which creates justice, but the flourishing of self-responsible well-being among a consentaneous people which gives rise to economic success.

From the point of view of pragmatic corporate-statism, however, economic success is not necessarily grounded in social success. It surely is not dependent upon ethical success. It equates only with political success. The strong are those that rule, which means, in the final analysis, those who are most manipulative, aggressive, and ruthlessly efficient (in inducing social conformity). It means that those that rule are the most fit; not that those most fit should rule.

But true justice is not conformity, state law, or submission to rule by force. Justice is not an authoritarian exercise in *ordering* human interaction, but a system of validating *just* forms of human interaction and condemning unjust ones. Authoritarian organizations which claim for themselves an understanding of what all human beings should do with their lives are merely apparatuses for *ordering human beings so to satisfy the selfish designs of those in power*; they are not political associations which work to achieve justice. Whether these rulers claim their right to rule because of fitness through strength, wealth, wisdom, religious piety, or social status, the fact remains that they demand authority over personal sovereignty, the power to define individual determination, and an exclusive knowledge of right and wrong action. They claim the right to define what justice is solely with respect to their own predispositions.

Justice is not an extension of the status quo; rather, it is an extension of the moral judgments of rational individuals. Justice cannot be found in the inanimate structure of the physical universe, or in the dusty passages of translated scripture, or in the whim of a single dictator, or in the opinions of a democratic mob. Justice is not part of the leadership/follower ethic at all; rather, it is a simple plea for sovereignty.

The goal of justice is not to enable the fit to survive. Rather, **the goal of justice is the survival of values.**

Law and the "Order of Consonance": Giving Justice Political Coherency

The concept of law, as a political extension of justice, initially grows out of ethical concerns. It must be consistent with (and thereby promote) voluntary association and the sovereignty of selves.

Law is the mechanism of giving justice political coherency and stability. Law is always to work *on the side of* justice, as an ordering element, for the protection of the individual and his cooperative, communal concerns.

The fear is that if the state is given the job of maintaining order, it will appropriate to itself the authority to define *what* that order should be. Once this is allowed, the next step would be to grant the state power to *create* order, because mere maintenance would not be sufficient. Naked totalitarianism need not ask for more.

The Gordian knot is cut by this insight: social justice is a product of the *universal interdependencies* of selfest values, of the mutual expansion of self-responsible sovereignty within a coherent and consentaneous community. Justice, or that which protects selfest values, is defined in terms of *universal* rights and reciprocity: the *universal* right to life and liberty, the *universal* fairness inherent in doing unto others only that which, if done to you, would promote your own sovreignty and personal dignity. Injustice, or that which confiscates selfest values, is defined in terms of rights transgressions and initial aggression: theft, destruction, fraud, intimidation with intent to manipulate or harm, etc. To rape, pillage, and plunder is unjust - not because the state so defines it; rather, these things are transgressions against the personal sovereignty of flesh and blood people. The state's task is not to create laws out of thin air that mandate, in turn, a Just Order; rather, it is to identify (recognize) the sovereignty that exists as separate human beings. Criminals are those who abridge this sovereignty by breaking the common and recognizable laws against unjust interaction.

Within the Politics of Rights, the legitimate state *protects* a social order of just action, but not by creating or self-defining that action. Rather, it does this by protecting the sovereignty of each citizen *against* transgressions both domestic and foreign. Political action need not, and should not, replace any existing mechanisms for such protection, but should merely fill any appropriate void.

The mechanisms of convenience, of politically expedient compromises and judiciary process, all of which evolve as one aspect among many within a culture, are the tools of republican governmental activity. As such, they delimit zealous enthusiasm by a healthy conservative attitude. But their ultimate effectiveness is not judged by convenience as such. Rather, it is judged by how they effect a total spirit of justice (how they protect the sovereign values of responsible individuals).

What legitimate government maintains, by ordering its own mechanisms under this concept of justice, is Freedom (in the comprehensive selfest-responsible sense). The harmonious, consentaneous order created by the just interactions of a sovereign people - what might be termed the Freeing Order of Social Consonance - is the proper goal of human justice. Law, by being an *extention* (and not an exclusive source) of justice, has but a single goal: a **dynamic, spontaneous Order of Consonance**. What is protected, and thereby promoted, is creativity within stability, sovereignty within a supportive community, personal fulfillment within the recognition of universal human dignity. Law becomes the fair rules for free development, disciplining voluntary interactions between communities, associations, and individuals.

As Garry Wills rightly pointed out in his wonderful essay, *The Convenient State*, "no nation *can* long endure if it is only 'dedicated to a proposition,'" especially if that proposition be a specific ordering of society by a single vision of Virtue. "It must be dedicated to a people," he continues, "to its particular human possibilities." This is at once a freeing and binding demand, a creative yet conservative insight, breathing life into the concept of law while at the same time limiting its scope.

As the codification of justice, law must remain dedicated to self-responsible personal sovereignty while remaining an extension of the infinitely human, cultural-bound, ever-changing Order of Consonance. It cannot become an instrument of illegitimate redistribution and regulation, a centralized moral authority, or a tool of hierarchical power. This is the real tension, and the real hope, of the modern world: Self-responsibility within Community. Law must be a disciplining element of that tension, while remaining a just product of that cherished hope.

When laws truly reflect this ethical premise, they will become worthy of allegiance. Until that time, they will remain a source of cynicism, division, and rebellion.

Part Three:

THE POLITICS OF RIGHTS

Part Three:
THE POLITICS OF RIGHTS

If "to govern" means "to rule," as in "controlling and directing others," then the proper role of political associations is *not* to govern (no matter what the etymology of "*govern*ment" might imply). Power, for a government bent on governing, will be employed mainly to seize, stifle, and exclude.

Most people would confess that if they had things their own way, they would just as soon be free of governmental intervention and compete on the open market like self-responsible individuals. But it is no longer so simple. Since So-and-so has an advantage because of this and that tariff and/or protective regulation, "equal opportunity" is demanded. Fair is fair, right? Democracy becomes a mechanism for the equal distribution of muck and misery.

> The manufacturer subsidized by the State with one throw of the dice is forced to pay above market wages with the next; and the union member's advantage is taxed away to help bail out a decaying industry. The doctor who is enriched by Medicare is forced to subsidize price support programs for tobacco and peanuts, while farmers underwrite New York's urban renewal. The welfare recipient pays a host of hidden taxes every time he makes a purchase, in order to support the welfare bureaucracy; and the bureaucrat, like everyone else, is forced to pay higher and higher prices for everything he buys because of State engineered inflation... (Edmund A. Opitz, from his introduction to Nock's *Our Enemy, The State*)

If the purpose of government is to govern society (which includes, of course, each individual) toward "society's best interests," no other outcome is possible. However, if society (that is, every individual within a multiplicity of supportive communities) was able to look out for itself, the result could be quite different. One of the purposes of THE POLITICS OF RIGHTS is to illustrate this difference.

If political associations are not meant to govern, it should be asked, what are they good for? The purpose of political associations is to protect individual rights and assist the dynamic and spontaneous harmony - the natural Order of Consonance - which develops between sovereign people.

Legitimate law is a codification of the *negative* obligations which promote self-responsibility, as opposed to a codification of positive ethical assertiveness. Politic action should not dictate what a man should *do* with his life, but only what he *cannot do* to others. To limit political demands to *negative* obligations helps to distinguish government's role as a *protector* of values, as opposed to a *maker of values*.

Since the protection of individual values often involves the use of force, political associations must have the authority to employ force, but they must also continually attempt to make force as uncoercive as possible. Force can never be used except for reasons of protection, as in the many extensions of self-defense (police aid, national defense, compulsory restitution, etc.) Political force is meant to keep individuals free so that they may pursue, unencumbered and in an air of rational certainty, their own responsible activities. Any use of force which undermines personal sovereignty and voluntary association is coercive and must be outlawed.

This implies that there is a difference between one kind of force and another. If political force does not harm the processes of voluntary association and the responsible self-determined actions of individuals, it is not specifically coercive force.

"Coercion," to use F. A. Hayek's definition, "implies both the threat of inflicting harm and the intention thereby to bring about certain conduct" (*The Constitution of Liberty*). Coercion is not merely force, but force used to manipulate another's will. This separates force used in *retaining* individual liberty (self-defensive force and all that implies) from the force used in *abridging* individual liberty.

Coercion is more than saber rattling and police brutality. In the age of modern psychology and drug use, in the age of state-sponsored education and democratic referendums and unlimited regulation, the concept of coercion takes on added significance. It is not merely strong-arming a citizenry. It is also any form of manipulation which undermines individual will. To quote Hayek further: "though the coerced still chooses, the alternatives are determined for him by the coercer so that he will choose what the coercer wants. . . He is not altogether deprived of his capacities; but he is deprived of the possibilities of using his knowledge for his own aims."

No government on earth limits itself to noncoercive force. In fact, modern government, thinking its broad aims are sanctified by majority will, believes that nearly *any* means can be employed to achieve that will. Any form of force, especially coercive force, is employed to increase government's functions and powers so to better establish this politically defined "majority will." In this manner, the force used by government no longer *serves* the individual by protecting his liberty and self-ownership. Instead, force becomes a tool to manipulate the individual into conforming to the ends government itself sets. Government becomes a coercive agent by the decree of the majority.

What was intended by the first theories of political liberty was that force should be abolished - except in its proper manifestation as a protector of the private spheres of action (including labor, trade, property, faith, family, etc.) These theorists were not anarchists who wanted to do away with government. Rather, they saw the importance of political institutions which promoted individual liberty. It was not power which was bad (power being the ability to achieve one's aims), but the power to coerce. "It is not power in the sense of an extension of our capacities which corrupts, but the subjection of other human wills to ours, the use of other men against their will for our purposes" (Hayek). Thus, liberty became the paramount object of political theory.

> Liberty and good government do not exclude each other; and there are excellent reasons why they should go together; but they do not necessarily go together. **Liberty is not a means to a higher political end. It is itself the highest political end.** It is not for the sake of a good public administration that it is required, but for the security in the pursuit of the highest objects of civil society, and of private life. (Lord Acton)

When liberty becomes the goal of government, people enjoy the freedom to employ the principles of voluntary association, the freedom to pursue their own ends, the freedom to fulfill their own human potential. This is not because liberty makes for effective government, but because liberty makes for effective individuals.

The U.S. Constitution and the federal system it delimited was one of the noblest experiments yet employed to protect individual liberty. That today our government requires permission for almost every economic activity (through certification, licensing, permits, regulations, disclosure laws, etc.), treats individual property as its own (through eminent domain laws, taxation, the regulation of production and labor activities, etc.), has created an increasing number of protected monopoly activities (in the fields of utilities, communications, transportation, resource management, labor unions, space exploration and utilization, etc.), and has intruded into the private lives of individuals in an attempt to cure their "vices" (through the criminalization of prostitution and homosexual activities, recreational drug use laws, gun control, etc.) - to mention only a few areas of coercive governmental intervention - is not really the fault of the Constitution and the political structure designed by the Founding Fathers. Their Constitution has been reconstructed through amendments, judicial discretion, the multiplying effect of precedence, and accumulating actions of political expediency. Essentially, what has been undermined is the *spirit* of the Constitution, the Higher Law of individual liberty that was meant to permeate and delimit all governmental action.

Political doctrine is not written in stone. Neither is it self-evident nor beyond passions and wants. It is a living reflection of the ethical philosophy practiced by the people involved. Our American system, designed to keep demagogues from throwing their own immoral weight onto powerless citizens, is grounded in a more basic ethical standard: that each man is to be self-powered and self-governing, within the rational context of inalienable rights. Just as your neighbor should not steal your property or abuse your person, so are you to be protected from institutional pillaging and coercion. The United States Constitution tries to minimize the possibility of both. Where it succeeds and where it fails are matters to be identified through experience and analysis. But the standard of success is ethical: Is each man more sovereign because of the political structure employed?

The wonderful critic of government, Henry David Thoreau, put it this way:

> The progress from an absolute to a limited monarchy, from a limited monarchy to a democracy, is a progress toward a true respect for the individual. Is a democracy, such as we know it, the last improvement possible in government? Is it not possible to take a step further towards recognizing and organizing the rights of man? There will never be a really free and enlightened State, until the State comes to recognize the individual as a higher authority and independent power, from which all its own power and authority are derived, and treats him accordingly. (*Civil Disobedience*)

The conflict to be waged is no longer republicanism versus monarchy or democracy versus communism, but liberty versus the strangling excesses of democracy itself.

THE POLITICS OF RIGHTS includes the following sections:
  The Concept of Rights
    Rights and Well-being
    Rights and the Moral Individual
    Rights: An Extension of "Ultimate Value"
    Property: An Extension of Self-ownership
    Property Rights as Basic Right
  The Allocation Principle
    The Allocation Process
    As a Test: Some Examples
    Limitation and Structure
  Spontaneous Consonance
    Public Opinion
      Social Order as Common Sense
      Society and Government as Separate Entities
      "Society as Criminal" Creates Need for Political Action
    Free Trade
      Commerce as Needs Satisfaction
      Needs Satisfaction vs. Legislative Mandates
    The Family
      The Concept of Trusteeship
      Property Rights and the Transfer of Trusteeship
  Proper Attributes of Political Associations
    The Allocation Principle and Rights Protection
    Isonomy: Equality of Law
    Predictability
    No Monopoly Powers
    Representation and Balance
    Restitution, Not Punishment
    Liability, Not Immunity
    Noncoercive Revenue
    In Conclusion
  Practicality and Progress
    Ignorance and Liberty
    Exploitation and Regulation
    Taming the Beast with Required Compensation
    The Free Life - The Good Life

THE CONCEPT OF RIGHTS

The only way to support a dynamic Order of Consonance is to insulate personal sovereignty with protective rights. If this is not done, social order is no longer a creation of the harmonious commerce and communication between free people, but an imposed stratification maintained by continual oppression.

Delimiting government becomes paramount when it is understood that political action does *not* itself create the conditions which enable sovereignty to develop. Rather, the Order of Consonance provides the environment in which people become self-governed. The many goals of human action must be provided by the internal motivations of individual moral agents. The accumulative effect is a strengthening of the community through cooperative self-responsibility, a spontaneous order which develops out of like needs and consonant aspirations. The only function legitimate political associations have is to provide mechanisms, when otherwise lacking, which protect the individual's responsible pursuit of his own well-being.

Rights and Well-being

Alan Gewirth has stated that a right is that which a person *must* do to achieve well-being. The "must" is what is crucial: a human being cannot be kept from doing that which he must do to achieve well-being - he must have an inalienable *right* to those "must" actions. This assertion seems perfectly consistent with a comprehensive demand for universal human dignity.

It is reasonable to assume that food, shelter, human association, creative and productive experiences, a certain degree of education, and a sane and ecologically sound environment are all things a person must have to achieve well-being. It would follow that it is a person's right to eat, sleep protected, interact creatively and productively with other human beings, pursue any knowledge to any degree which satisfies, live in a sane and ecologically sound community, and expect a conservative amount of surety and continuity in the social order.

The implications of this stance immediately call into question the obligations one citizen has in accommodating another's well-being. Everyone must have the right to eat one's own food. However, if an individual is destitute and starving, must others provide him with food? Is it his *right* to be provided for? If he is not provided for, is it his right to steal? If he is not destitute yet refuses to eat, should he be force fed? Does it make a difference if his refusal to eat is a rational statement of protest? What if his refusal to eat is tied to a personal decision to commit suicide? What if it is due to a treatable disease or neurosis? What if the disease is untreatable? What if the individual is mentally incompetent? Can "well-being" even be defined in any objective fashion when incompetence is involved? Where does the paternalism stop? Should it have limits at all?

The "must" actions in Gewirth's definition of rights must be of a specific kind: actions an *individual* must do to achieve well-being. Rights cannot be what *others* must do to assist in this achievement. In other words, the most basic right is the freedom of action to pursue well-being: personal sovereignty.

What is important from a social perspective is that the concept of rights entails a freedom to *do* something, not to have something done for you. If the concept of rights is to be a universally valid concept, one person's rights cannot impose a positive obligation on others to provide for him in any compulsory manner.

Regarding the right to procure one's own food, this would entail the right to productive work, to voluntary trade, to live off of one's savings and surplus, to seek loans, etc. It also implies that, for the destitute and unemployed, begging for charity in any consentual manner is one's right. When sought on a personal level, charity (which, in a selfest scenario, is akin to compassionate value-investments in the destitutes' human dignity and potential sovereignty) is rarely refused out of one's own surplus. And the beggar, responsibly so, should promise restitution as soon as possible (even if the contribution is freely given), because the beggar must consider the benevolent action of charity as a good-faith loan.

What would happen if none of these avenues of voluntary activities procures enough food for sufficient sustenance?

There is a good case to be made for the right of the starving to steal for their supper, after all other avenues have been pursued. It would seem that any other alternative condemns the starving to a silent death at the hands of an affluent and apathetic elite (if such affluence exists). If emergency theft became a protected right (yet one that would be rarely recognized within the judicial process, since complete destitution and a comprehensive history of seeking out alternative methods for procuring food would be difficult to prove), the rational reaction of a responsible community would be to develop its productive self-sufficiency on the one hand and to set up well publicized charity centers on the other. Such a productive and caring community would thus circumvent any need for emergency thefts. All theft could then be outlawed in good conscience and a sane environment could be preserved. (Note that even this scenario is *not* a sanction for a welfare state, since charity would still be voluntary and self-responsibility would still be at a premium.)

Wouldn't such a system give license to the destitute and their representatives to utilize what might be termed "extortion by need"? Consider the contradiction of a starving man pounding on the doors of a shop owner, demanding either a job or food, while the shop owner points a rifle at him from a second story window, exclaiming how he is barely making ends meet as is. Both men are pursuing their own well-being by protecting their own survival and property. Both men are acting within their rights, yet they have come into infinite conflict. On whose side should local authorities intervene? This contradiction prompted Gewirth to state,

> Universal ethical egoism requires that the egoist take impartially the position of each person acting for his own respective self-interest and that he have the criterion of his "oughts" reflect their respective self-interests, even when this is opposed to his own self-interest as an agent. **As an egoist, he must advocate *for* his own self-interest; as a *universal* egoist, he must advocate others' acting *against* his own self-interest when theirs conflicts with his.** *(Gewirth's Ethical Rationalism)*

The social chaos such a "license by need" would create is nowhere more apparent than in Jean Raspail's chilling french novel, *In the Camp of the Saints*. In it, legions of impoverished, starving people attack the wealth of the West. Destitute blacks revolt in America. Millions of hungry orientals invade Russia. And out of Calcutta comes a pathetic convoy, a refugee fleet of a hundred dilapidated ships on which millions of Indians crouch, bound for Europe, for "paradise," ready to break the dyke between Western prosperity and Third World poverty. In the end, by demanding only sustenance, these legions of poor "peacefully" overrun the altruistically paralyzed West, at the same time bringing about the downfall of civilization. After confronting this powerful analogy, it is easy to see how the concept of emergency theft might lead to not only irresponsible abuse on an individual level, but intercommunity violence and international war.

The right to emergency theft must be maintained, but only when legitimized by the following conditions: (1) The individual in question cannot be directly responsible for his own destitution (else he himself has caused the situation which legitimizes his emergency theft, which would be a matter of either extreme irresponsibleness or simple premeditated theft). (2) Enough appropriate and consentaneous attempts have been made by the individual to procure sustenance as to reasonably exhaust his possibilities for nontransgressive action. (3) The act of emergency theft (a) cannot cause the destitution of other innocent people, and (b) must be directed against the coercive forces, if appropriate, that have caused the breakdown of peaceful, sane, productive commerce or are presently repressing the possibility of nonaggressive procurement.

It is difficult to imagine a scenario in which emergency theft is legitimate except in the case where a dynamic Order of Consonance has been replaced by a state of repressive or outright chaos due to governmental/criminal intervention or natural catastrophe. If the social environment is so monopolized by anti-ethical interdependencies, so closed or chaotic that the individual is not free to act in an ethical manner consonant with his well-being, then aggressive action becomes for him his only survival outlet. Of course, the individual can always choose passive inaction over aggressive action, but when the consequence of inaction is death, passivity loses its appeal. When there are no ethical alternatives, justice is impossible and laws are but a barricade against survival.

> The reason that rights appear only when reasonably sane societal conditions prevail, and not in emergency and purely chaotic situations, is that one person, say

> Jones, can only have rights against another, say Smith, to the extent that condemnable actions against Jones by Smith are necessary to Smith's well-being. **The key feature of reasonably sane societal conditions is that they provide each person with multiple and non-condemnable means of seeking his own well-being.** (Erik Mack, "Egoism and Rights", *The Personalist*, 1973 Winter, pp.5-33)

On the bright side, if the the lack of sane and open societal conditions can be traced to specific oppressive agents, then emergency theft becomes a legitimate act of self-defense and a form of "freedom fighting" against an oppressive regime. In such a case, fighting for survival nicely coincides with the ethical fight for social justice.

When reasonably sane and open societal conditions exist, all manner of transgressions are an immoral theft of another's values.

This same line of reasoning is able to resolve the otherwise irresolvable contradictions regarding paternalistic actions. As John Hospers argues (in "Libertarianism and Legal Paternalism"): if a friend attempts suicide, it is well and proper for you to intervene. But your purpose is not to impose your will upon your friend; rather, it is to make sure your friend is acting for his own well-being. It may be that, after considering the matter, your friend still wishes to die. That would be his right (well-being is not merely a physical concept, but a comprehensive psychological one as well). Then again, your friend may reconsider and choose to live. Your act of emergency paternalism provided him with a second chance. Far from breaching his self-responsibility, you have helped maintain it and even augmented it. A great value - your friend's life - has been protected all the way around. And everyone's true sovereignty is preserved.

Using the standard of self-responsible sovereignty, every category of "must" actions can be properly analyzed. Whether it be shelter, associations, education, health, or the environment, an individual must remain free to pursue the conditions of well-being, but this freedom cannot include an obligation on others to provide.

Of course, there are many conditions for well-being that others could not provide even if they were so inclined or so commanded. For example, it would obviously be conducive to one's well-being to love and be loved in return. But emotion cannot be legislated in any matter. Society cannot force one person to love another; it cannot demand that love be reciprocated; it cannot even provide a suitable object for one to love in all cases; and, surely, it cannot create in a man the source of love if he is naturally hardhearted. All an individual has a protected right to is the act of loving: he must be free to love whom or what he desires.

The same argument can be made regarding education. A structure of schooling can be compulsory (as is presently the case), but actual *learning* is a complex interaction between the individual and his environment which mere structure cannot induce. The right to pursue learning does not include compulsory attendance at government schools; it would, however, include protection from compulsory ignorance forced upon children by an aberrant parent or community.

Consider the importance of a sane community. If a social environment is chaotic and insane, the mere demand for an individual's "right" to sane surroundings would not be sufficient cause for order and sanity to automatically occur. All that can be protected is the individual's right to *pursue* a sane and secure community, to escape and search for a community more conducive to his well-being, or found a new one on his own.

Lastly, consider the issue of incompetence. Do the inabilities of the mentally incompetent to achieve even the state of self-responsibility change this equation for rights? No. Their need cannot create a positive obligation in the form of political rights. Rights merely protected them from initial aggression. Simple compassion might infer community obligation of some sort, but this obligation stems from personal sentiment, from an individual sense of brotherhood and communal responsibility, not any predatory rights the incompetent might possess. It behooves a community to care for all its members who do not have the capacity to care for themselves in a dignified fashion, supporting their well-being as much as is appropriate while nurturing any potential sovereignty. But such care is grounded in good conscience, not political rights.

In the end, well-being is seen as a subjective state that is beyond objective definition, beyond universal legislation, sometimes even beyond achievement. Well-being itself cannot be a universal standard for rights; rather, it is the freedom to pursue well-being which must be protected: self-responsible sovereignty.

Rights and the Moral Individual

In order to further refine the concept of rights, it must be specifically differentiated from demands society levies on the individual within the potentially compromising process of community living. However compelling these social obligations may seem, they are not of the same genus as rights.

"Rights" must define an individual sphere of self-possession and self-power, differentiating it from any other person's sphere. In a social context, this becomes a **limit on action**, limiting any action which would transgress that individual sphere - or infringe one's "rights."

Why should an individual sphere of self-possession and self-power by defined? First, such a sphere is morally necessary within a less than perfect social context. Second, if rights are not coherently defined, they are not coherently defensible. The moral individual would then be at the intellectual (and political) mercy of the community at large.

> "Rights" are a moral concept - the concept that provides a logical transition from the principles guiding an individual's actions to the principles guiding his relationship with others - the concept that preserves and protects individual morality in a social context - the link between the moral code of a man and the legal code of a society, between ethics and politics. *Individual rights are the means of subordinating society to moral law.* (Ayn Rand, "Man's Rights", *The Virtue of Selfishness*)

The concept of rights, by insolating the private sphere of moral action, would not create a national creed of any specific order (as might be implied by Rand's comments). Of course, codifying responsible sovereignty *would*, in a way, be an assertion of "moral law." But it would be of a completely different nature than what might be codified into law by other moralities. Adherence to individual rights could not bring society under any *coercive* "moral law." It would merely protect the moral individual from being abused in any manner.

> For the individual, a right is a moral sanction of a *positive* - of his freedom to act on his own judgment, for his own goals, by his own *voluntary, uncoerced* choice. As to his neighbors, his rights impose no obligations on them except as a *negative* kind: to abstain from violating his rights... A right does not include the material implementation of that right by other men; it includes only the freedom to earn that implementation by one's own effort... Rights are moral principles which define and protect a man's freedom of action, but impose no obligations on other men. (Rand)

The notion of "positive obligation" must be purged from the concept of rights. If it is not, rights not only fail to protect one person from domination by another, they would demand that domination be the order of the day.

Rights: An Extension of the "Ultimate Value"

The concept of rights must, in practice, protect specific values which adhere to the individual. The natural foundation for these values is the ultimate human value: life.

Why is life an "ultimate" value? Because there is no value which can supersede it. There is no "higher" value. All other legitimate values (and, thus, necessary rights) are based on this ultimate value.

"Life" is the only phenomenon that is an end in itself: a value gained and kept by a constant process of goal-oriented (and, thus, value-oriented) action. But each of those value-oriented actions, indeed, the very concept of "value," is generically dependent upon and derived from the antecedent concept of "life." Douglas Rasmussen clarifies:

> "Life is an end in itself: a value gained and kept by a constant process of action." These words are absolutely crucial, for they show that living being is inherently value-laden. Yet, this does not make life

an intrinsic value - a value that is not an object of some entity's action. On the contrary, the relational nature of value - the idea that something becomes valuable not only because of its characteristics but also because it is an object of an entity's actions - is preserved in saying life is a value in itself, for living being is the entire complex of relation that makes something a value. **Living being acts to live. It is, itself, both the terms of the relation as well as the relation itself. This is what it means to be an end in itself. This type of being does not require anything else to justify its status as a value, for its being a value is what it is.** ("Groundwork for Rights", a critique of Rand's concept of rights, published in *The Personalist*, Winter 1980)

If the concept of rights is to protect the sphere of individual action a person *must* possess in order to achieve and maintain necessary values, then **man's life as a moral end in itself is the ultimate value rights are to defend.** It follows that anything which threatens or harms the concept of man as a moral end in himself (coercion, conformity, credulity) is an *enemy* of rights.

In summary, one *must* be free (physically and intellectually) to perform actions which attain and sustain one's life-making values. These "must" actions become one's "rights." Thus, the two founding principles of rights, one a corollary of the other, become: (1) **the right to life, which, in a socio-political context, translates into the right to self-ownership, and (2) the right to freedom from coercion.** To act within one's rights is to take responsibility for one's self-ownership. To violate another's rights is to compel someone to act against his own well-being or to appropriate his values.

All other rights are merely extensions and clarifications of these two ethical principles. I will refer to them from now on simply as "first rights."

Property: An Extension of Self-ownership

According to many dogmas, possessing property is a major impediment to individual fulfillment, a kind of immoral materialistic temptation, a source of greed and envy which finds its roots in inequality. These dogmas condemn property as an evil in itself (as if the human greed that misuses it would not have other outlets of coercion if private property did not exist). They end up either outlawing the private possession of property (as in communism) or branding it as a necessary evil that must be regulated for the general welfare of the human race (as in the administration of Social Democracy). Both views do great damage to the humane significance of inviolate private property.

The legally recognized concept of property is perhaps the most useful clarification of "first rights." A recognition of property rights aids the recognition of one's rights to self-ownership and freedom from coercion by defining *exactly* what one's private sphere of self-possession and self-power is, making that sphere *synonymous* with one's property. Property rights, being a fairly easy concept to define and legally enforce (as opposed to other more elusive rights, such as religious rights or the right to free speech), becomes the tangible mechanism for protecting "first rights."

The first step is to define property.

The initial property which is one's own is one's *body*. This is explicit in the concept of self-ownership. But it must also extend into all *labor* which the self performs, as well as all previously unowned *materials* one takes and reshapes with one's labor. John Locke provided the classic argument three hundred years ago:

> Every man has a "property" in his own "person." This nobody has any right to but himself. The "labour" of his body and the "work" of his hands, we may say, are properly his. Whatsoever, then, he removes out of the state that Nature hath provided and left in, he hath mixed his labour with it, and joined to it something that is his own, and thereby makes it his property. It being by him removed from the common state Nature placed it in, it hath by his labour something annexed to it that excludes the

Property: An Extension of Self-ownership

common right of other men. For this "labour" being the unquestionable property of the labourer, no man but he can have a right to what that is once joined to...

He that is nourished by the acorns he picked up under an oak, or the apples he gathered from the trees in the woods, has certainly appropriated them to himself. Nobody can deny but the nourishment is his. I ask, then, when did they begin to be his? when digested? or when he ate? or when he boiled? or when he brought them home? or when he picked them up? And it is plain, if the first gathering made them not his, nothing else could. That labour put a distinction between them and common. That added something to them more than Nature... and so they became his private right. And will anyone say he had no right to those acorns or apples he thus appropriated because he had not the consent of all mankind to make them his? Was it robbery thus to assume to himself what belonged to all in common [in the state of Nature]? If such a consent as that was necessary, the man [would have] starved not-withstanding the plenty God had given him. We see in commons, which remain so by compact, that it is the taking any part of what is common, and removing it out of the state Nature leaves it in, which begins the property, without which common is of no use. And the taking of this or that part does not depend on the express consent of all commoners. Thus, the grass my horse bit, the turfs my servant has cut, and the ore I have digged in any place, where I have a right to them in common with others, becomes my property without the assignation or consent of anybody. The labour that was mine, removing them out of that common state they were in, hath fixed my property in them. (*II Civil Government*, V, 26-27)

One's body, one's labor, and all materials taken from the "state of Nature" by one's labor or the labor of one's agents are defined as private property. This serves as a good starting point. But in modern society, most ownership is determined by a combination of labor and private property exchanges. It would seem consistent with the right of possession that any voluntary exchange of property can be added to our list. Therefore, any property, legitimately owned by one party, attained by another party through a *voluntary exchange* of that person's legitimately owned property, must now be included in the receiving party's definition of legitimate property. Following this reasoning, legitimate property received as a *gift* must be on the list as well, since the right of possession includes the right to determine subsequent ownership without asking for any exchange in return.

Regarding property exchanges, the concept of "legitimacy" must be specifically defined. Obviously, property obtained through coercion would *not* be legitimate. Thus, one does not have the right of use and disposal of property obtained through theft, fraud, or extortion. One *does* have the right of use and disposal of all *legitimately obtained* property. Only legitimate property born out of the "common" with one's labor or received through some sort of voluntary exchange (trade or gift) becomes one's own legitimate property.

What about stolen property which was sold to you without your knowledge of its illegitimacy? Does that make a difference? Wouldn't it be property obtained through a voluntary exchange? Yes, the property in question was obtained in a voluntary exchange, but not in an exchange of *legitimate* property. No amount of voluntary exchanges can make illegitimate property legitimate. The problem becomes one of sorting out the history of ownership and exchanges for a specific piece of property. One can only own legitimate property rights to property obtained from a legitimate owner. If no legitimate owner exists for a particular item then it must become a part of the "common" again. No one can have initial claim to it.

To underscore the importance of property rights, Locke understood the very purpose of civil government - that institution explicitly designated to protect all individual rights - to be the protection of individually obtained property, for *in that protection all other rights were protected*. This same conviction dominates libertarian-conservative political theory today.

> Since material goods are produced by the mind and effort of individual men, and are the result of his effort, and are needed to sustain their lives, if the producer does not own the result of his effort, he does not own his own life. **To deny property rights means to turn men into property owned by the state.** Whoever claims the "right" to "redistribute" the wealth produced by others is claiming the "right" to treat human beings as chattel. (Ayn Rand, "The Monument Builders", *The Virtue of Selfishness*)

The "right" of property ownership is properly understood as an extension of the right to self-ownership.

> **The right to property is the right of use and disposal.** If one is not free to use that which one has produced, one does not possess the right of liberty. If one is not free to make the products of one's work serve one's chosen goals, one does not possess the right to the pursuit of happiness. And - since man is not a ghost who exists in some non-material manner - if one is not free to keep and to consume the products of one's work, one does not possess the right of life. (Nathanial Branden, *The Objectivist Newsletter*, Vol. 1, No. 2, February 1962)

It is the ethical right to pursue one's ultimate value, *life*, which demands that one possess property rights. This ethical "first right" also defines what property rights must be: the right of "use and disposal of one's property." Without this right, the rights to liberty, to pursuing happiness, and to life itself lose all meaning.

The existence of property rights is also the greatest protection against any abuse of one's "first rights." They are what protect us from slavery. They protect us from theft, fraud, and extortion. And they protect us from that most dangerous of coercers: government. It is only when our property rights are abridged or when exceptions are made to them that we lose our grip on liberty and on our very lives.

THE NEW AGE POLITICS

Property Rights and Free Trade. In an age when a call for "human rights" and "civil rights" often becomes synonymous with economic intervention and governmental regulation, it must be explicitly restated how the right of use and disposal of one's legitimate property demands the freedom to market and exchange one's property in any manner which does not infringe upon another's rights, just as the ethical principle of voluntary association demands such a free economic system. If one has the right of possession, one must have the right of voluntary exchange. In fact, one has the right *not* to be involved in any coercive economic order which would require an abridgement of property rights.

> Every man, as long as he does not violate the laws of justice, is left perfectly free to pursue his own interest his own way, and bring both his industry and capital into competition with those of any other man, or order of men. (Adam Smith, *An Inquiry into the Nature and Causes of the Wealth of Nations*, Bk. IV, Ch. 9)

> After all, what is Competition? Is it a thing which exists and is self-acting like the cholera? No, Competition is only the absence of constraint. In what concerns my own interests, I desire to choose for myself, not that another should choose for me, or in spite of me - that is all. And if one pretends to substitute his judgment for mine in what concerns me, I should ask to substitute mine for his in what concerns him. What guarantee have we that things would go on better in this way? It is evident that Competition is Liberty. To take away the liberty of acting is to destroy the possibility, and consequently the power, of choosing, of judging, of comparing: it is to annihilate intelligence. To annihilate thought, to annihilate man. From whatever quarter they set out, to this point all modern reformers tend - to ameliorate society they begin by annihilating the individual, under the pretext that all evils come from

this source - as if all good did not come from it too.
(Frederic Bastiat, *Harmonies of Political Economy*, Ch. 10)

To deny men free trade is to deny them their property rights. To deny men property rights is to deny them their right to life, liberty, and the pursuit of well-being. To deny men life, liberty, and the pursuit of well-being is to deny them the required values that make them human beings. To deny them this is to deny men dignity, purpose, and meaning.

Property rights are the fundamental problem of political theory precisely because they are the fundamental social manifestation of the ultimate ethical principle: that each person is an end in himself, is his own ultimate value, and must pursue his well-being by the labor of his own mind and his own hands. They are the fundamental political embodiment of the universal principle of human dignity.

Property Rights as Basic Right

Property rights are not only the most fundamental legal rights which must be recognized to protect life and liberty. They are also properly seen as the more generic form of most all other rights.

The Bill of Rights delineates several rights which the United States government is supposed to recognize as inherent in each individual. These include religious tolerance, the freedom of speech and the press, the right to petition, the right to bear arms, the right to control who stays in your own house and to be protected from unwarranted searches and seizures, the right to due process, etc. We have come to view these rights as a multiplicity of distinct liberties, unconnected, each separately identified and protected. This has caused all of these rights to be abridged and transformed.

It is theoretically correct to state that all legal rights stem from the "first rights" of self-ownership and freedom from coercion. Practically speaking, however, property rights are the only legal rights which can coherently and consistently protect these "first rights." It is *within* the concept of property rights that such activities as free speech and religious tolerance are protected. When separate rights are *understood* as something *outside* of and distinct from property rights, great damage can be done.

Consider the problem of the "right" to free speech. Does this right protect any person to speak on whatever topic in whatever manner wherever he wants? Is he free to yell "fire!" in a crowded theatre, stand on his chair in a well-to-do restaurant and rhapsodize about Marxism, or stop traffic while he hands out leaflets advertising the grand opening of his uptown business? Surely not. But how do we define the right to free speech if not with respect to the freedom of speech itself? If one is not free to speak anywhere about anything, then is the right to free speech a limited right? Who sets the limit? Government, of course. And what happens is that the right to free speech is no longer a right but a prescribed privilege defined by the state.

The same is true of religious tolerance. If a person's religious faith demands that he carry a poisonous snake around his neck down Main Street, is he protected by the Constitution to do so? If his religion dictates he evangelize from door to door daily, calling on the same houses over and over until the inhabitants are converted, is he protected by the Constitution to do so? If not, wouldn't such a limitation be an infringement on his religious rights? Must religious tolerance be defined within "socially proper limits"? Who does the defining? Government, of course.

Both of these "rights" can be distilled into the concept of property rights. In the case of free speech, the theatre and restaurant owners are the property holders and can require any noncoercive code of conduct within their establishments, due to their right of use and disposal of their property. Thus, someone cannot misuse their establishment. A person would be infringing upon the owner's property rights if he yelled fire or stood up on a chair and began preaching (if that was not tolerable to the owner). Also, if the street in question were owned by an individual, a neighborhood coalition, or a community/municipal association, then those owners would determine if people could distribute leaflets on their property. They could license them accordingly and maintain a contractual responsibility for their behavior. In this way, safety, civility, liability, and rights remain clearly defined. There is no need to alienate rights from the individual and no one is coerced.

In the case of religious tolerance, the same argument holds true. An individual is free to do with his mind and body whatever he pleases, so long as it does not infringe upon anyone else's rights. Obviously, carrying a dangerous snake in public threatens the well-being of others and should be outlawed. The basis for this is the right to life that each person possess: the property rights to his own body. Likewise, an individual can decide who can come to his door and who will be turned away. An evangelist has no "religious rights," per se. He has only those property rights which protect him from abuse and transgressions by others. He is free, within the protection of property rights, to worship whom he wants in any noncoercive manner he wants within his own church and house and within his own mind.

Separating out specific rights from the generic concept of property rights causes them to be transformed into privileges defined by the government. They can no longer be inherent, inalienable, unabridgeable rights upon which no one, including government, can morally or legally infringe.

> It is impossible to look upon a man as free, so long as others have unlimited command over his property. It is impossible to separate the rights of actions from the rights of acquiring and possessing. A man acts through and by means of the various substances of the world, and if he is not free to acquire and own these substances as an individual, neither is he free to act as an individual. (Auberon Herbert)

Property Rights and Property Dispersal. The recognition of property rights is essential in the prevention of coercion in that it delimits the personal sphere of influence of individuals. It leaves each person his own oasis of self-power. But in modern society, where many individuals do not own their land and home and few own the business for which they work, the question of property rights may not be broad enough to completely protect one's "first rights."

F. A. Hayek has observed that the essential requisite to prevent coercion is not simply *owning* property, but that "the material means which enable [an individual] to pursue any plan of action should not be all in the exclusive control of one agent." Property ownership must be spread out and no one can have a monopoly on any particular function of survival. If this is the case, even a person with practically no property can be free if he can freely contract his services and interactions with others who do. "It is **competition made possible by the dispersion of property** that **deprives the individual owners of particular things of coercive powers**" (*The Constitution of Liberty*).

In other words, if only one man owns all the apartment buildings in an area and will not let you room in any of them, by exercising his property rights he can effectively cause you to freeze to death due to your inability to find shelter. Better yet, imagine your town if 90% were owned by two or three Mafia families, including all roads and water resources. The concept of inviolate property rights could then be used to support unscrupulous manipulation on the part of the Mafia families and destroy the well-being of the unpropertied. Such extreme examples (yet ones which parallel the situation in many countries - especially if government agents are included as a propertied class), illustrate Hayek's insight that the unpropertied can only be protected by the concept of property rights if enough people own property, so that the unpropertied can find someone among them to contract with.

What happens when property is consolidated into a few hands? Usually, this leads to totalitarian actions, either on the side of predatory redistribution for the "good of the people" or to a totalitarian manipulation of the people for the "good of the owner class." Neither option is acceptable within the concept of "first rights."

This is what must first be established: a social and economic system of voluntary association - free commerce devoid of extortion, fraud, and any exploitive manipulation. Such a system must be supported by a legal structure which protects all legitimate property. When such a system is put into place, the legal structure can begin to put all property to the test of legitimacy, and, in many nations around the globe, much of the land and means of production would be uncovered as illegitimate. This property would then be part of the "common." Legitimate claims would follow. Those who were directly mixing their labor with specific materials and assets would be presented with ownership. Buying and selling of newly acquired property and a boom in entrepreneurship would follow, all under the protection of the law of "first rights."

To the zealous reformer, this might seem like an intolerably conservative and slow approach. But the increase in wealth and the increase in social pluralism in such a progressively grounded society would proceed more rapidly and more securely than under any other restructuring plan. On the other hand, to those who sympathize with aristocratic landowners, this may seem like an intolerably radical land reform scheme. Yet, it is the only way to effect equalitarian justice without requiring Maoist tactics of forced relocation, widespread starvation, witch hunts of the wealthy.

The process of opening up a monopolistic society must not become a gallery of socio-political manipulation or governmental exploitation. If this were to happen, the entire concept of rights would be destroyed. Individuals would remain a means to someone else's selfish ends. Rights would be nothing more than a legislative creation, a species of the state, a thing penned by new rulers for their new subjects. There would be no necessary connection between political action and ethical justice. An Order of Consonance would not result.

Whenever reform is discussed, it becomes painfully apparent that procedures alone cannot create desired social consequences. A people must be ready to assert their own sovereignty; personal sovereignty cannot be created by legislation or animated through police action. The society itself must be on the side of true self-responsible justice, else any experiment in rights protection is forever doomed.

THE ALLOCATION PRINCIPLE

"First rights" are to supersede the imperfect particulars of everyday legislation. They must operate as an ever-present Higher Law - limiting, correcting, advising. In practice, however, legislative prerogative and judicial precedence are the actual standards regarding the administration of justice. How then is this Higher Law to be recognized?

Precedence itself cannot deflect the course of law; it can only perpetuate it. And in perpetuating it, leaders perpetuate their own leadership. To challenge the incorrectness of certain laws, dissenters are often forced to work *outside* the system, becoming criminals (conscientious objectors) in order to demonstrate the immorality of a certain judicial stance through martyrdom (civil disobedience). Pressure can then be exerted within the system to redirect the otherwise "closed" course of law. The problem with civil disobedience is that it relies on the sympathy and ethicality of those in power and, therefore, has only a limited effect. In addition, democratic procedure is difficult to harness (witness the many failed attempts to limit or decrease the growth of modern government).

As legislators attempt to deal with the daily complaints and needs of the electorate, laws are passed which address one issue while creating new and unforeseen complications. Other laws are passed in order to impose a particular vision of the future on society. As government delegates powers among its own members to better effect this vision, thousands and millions of particular laws are amassed. In the process, the Higher Law is either righteously dismissed as too restrictive or simply ignored.

Such a process is drowning democratic man beneath the ever-increasing flood of governmental regulation and lawmaking. It is time to drain the swamp.

A very simple and logical principle can be drawn from the concept of "first rights" which subjects all actions and powers of a particular association to a test of ethical legitimacy. This is what I have called **The Allocation Principle.**

The Allocation Principle

The Allocation Principle simply states:

> **(1) An individual or group of individuals can act only on the authority of self-held individual rights or on the authority of rights allocated to them by another individual, and (2) an individual can allocate to another individual or group of individuals only those rights which he himself possesses.**

What this principle does is set up a concrete standard for determining if a particular act is legitimate with respect to the ethical antecedent: self-ownership. If it is not, then that action is illegitimate.

Regarding the structure of political associations, The Allocation Principle demands that definite authority for all powers assumed and actions taken come directly from the rights of sovereign individuals. It demands that the authority of a particular agent or official or group be derived from individual people for the expressed purpose of protecting specific rights. It states that rights can be allocated from one person to another so to effect that protection and that no other assignment or appropriation of legitimate authority for political action exists.

Being a "servant of the people" does not endow government agents with special rights to coerce, initiate violence, or direct society toward a specific vision. Only individuals possess legitimate rights; only they can allocate these rights to others in the process of rights protection. Political associations have no rights of their own; they have only power.

It is this power - and this lack of inherent rights - which is so dangerous to a society, and which The Allocation Principle, if incorporated into the political mechanism on a constitutional level, would expose and delimit.

The Allocation Process

An individual allocates his rights to others so that he can better protect those rights. This allocation process does not alienate the individual from his rights in any manner; no transfer of ownership takes place, only an augmentation of responsible action.

Consider the right to self-defense. Criminals are often quite brutal and well armed. The right to self-defense can be allocated to specific agents (such as private bodyguards) in order to counteract this potential brutality. After a crime has been committed, aid is required to prosecute and gain restitution from one's transgressors. Policemen, law firms, arbitration courts, private investigators, and insurance companies might all be employed. But the legitimacy of their actions is derived from only one source: the rights of the individual. No other rights exist. No other source of legitimate authority exists.

The Allocation Principle does not define a specific process for allocating rights. It merely subjects that process to a test: all powers and functions of a political agent or association must be derived from specific rights allocated to them by specific individuals. If no individual has allocated his right(s) to the agent or association in question, then that agent or institution has no legitimate claim to authority. If no individual has a right to a particular action, then no group of individuals (like city hall) can assume that right.

As a Test: Some Examples

From where do political institutions derive their authority to make and enforce laws? They derive this authority from the rights of individuals who require laws so to protect their lives and properties.

What are the conditions which make these laws legitimate? The Allocation Principle would suggest: (1) that they are made by *known* delegates of the individuals who require such laws (so that the individuals can be certain *to whom* they are allocating this right); (2) that the laws pertain only to the protection of those rights in question (so that political institutions do not allocate to themselves illegitimate rights); (3) that these laws are equalitarian in nature, in that they pertain equally to all the citizenry (including the drafters and enforcers of that law), extend privilege to none, and abridge no one's legitimate rights (retaining the universal character of the concept of "first rights"); (4) the law must be specific in what action is to be declared unlawful (so that breaking the law can be planned for and avoided by normal action within one's private sphere); and (5) that any force required in enforcing the laws or in gaining restitution for the breaking of the laws be described in sufficient detail (so that an individual is protected against retaliatory force in excess to the crime committed).

Consider the impact the adoption of this principle would have, generally, on our present democratic system:

No agent could be delegated authority without the direct consent of the citizenry. This would make unlawful any extension of government authority or tax increase without specific electorate consent, as well as illegitemize any bureaucratic or police function not directly under the control of a chosen representative.

No law could be legitimate if it violated the universal rights of possession and private action. This would outlaw all legislation meant to regulate commerce, redistribute wealth, seize legitimate property, forcibly bus students, or in any way institute a specific "vision" for society through coercive intervention (although ecological and third party health related regulation would be permissible - see pp. 130, 155).

No agent could be given powers of discretion in determining to whom a law should pertain and to whom it should not, or what exactly any nonspecific law might mean. If a law required such a determination, it should be declared inadequate and returned to the legislature. This would curtail the powers of many judges (especially in the area of education rulings, separation of church and state issues, and other noncriminal cases) as well as the power of the Supreme Court to define legislative intent.

Consider a second example. From where does the government derives its authority to keep a standing army? This authority is derived from individuals who are threatened by various international camps, from small bands of terrorists to huge enemy armies. If no enemies existed, their would be no threat, and the need for an army would disappear. Within the foreseeable future, however, such threats exist, so a standing army is needed. Citizens afraid for their life and property, can allocate to specific agents, both professional and amateur, the authority to guard the general boarders of this nation.

But this authority does not include intervention into conflicts which do not pertain to the specific rights of a citizenry. In the case of the United States, an individual's right to self-defense does not necessarily translate into our government financing and manning NATO positions, actively protecting the Orient, funding dubious resistance movements with tax dollars, etc. Overseas agencies should be able to solicit help from our private citizens, but the professional agencies charged with the responsibility of protecting *our* citizens' rights cannot police the world for the sake of others' rights. The only reason for foreign intervention would be to stop aggression before it spills on to our shores. In such a case, prudent self-interest seems the best standard. Yet, prudence must acknowledge that every action has its consequence. It is within the rights of other nations, from their point of view, to arm themselves and strike back in an appropriate manner.

In addition, authority embodied in a standing army does not include the right to draft nonconsenting citizens or the power to demand a specific term of employment. One person's right to self-defense does not include another person's obligation to protect him. If an individual wishes to take up the allocated right of defending another person (or a nation of people), that is his individual choice. But one person's need does not create the authority for compulsion or coercion. Any army must at all times be voluntary. A compulsory draft, or any compulsory service to the state, no matter how temporary, is nothing less than slavery, an obvious assault on an individual's "first rights."

Lastly, consider the issue of taxation. From where does government derive its authority to tax? Can it claim that right merely because it can think of no other way of paying for its functions? Does authority come from the needs and desires and lack of creative entrepreneurship of lawmakers and law enforcers?

No, authority can only come from the rights of individuals. To show how The Allocation Principle simplifies such issues, it must be asked: who allocated to the tax collector the right to take income from taxed individuals? Do *I* have a right to my neighbor's income? Surely not. The right couldn't have come from me. Who then? The answer, of course, is "from no one." Taxation is an illegitimate power of government. Divested of its self-proclaimed authority, the tax collector is seen as what he truly is: a highway robber! If government, as a civilian association dedicated to individual sovereignty and a dynamic

Order of Consonance, needs money, it must get it in a more *civil* manner. (See "Noncoercive Revenue," pp. 143-147 below.)

It is often argued that the Order of Consonance requires government to possess the power of eminent domain and taxation so that it can use force to satisfy a communal need that would otherwise go unsatisfied. Indeed, the progressive preservation or expansion of a community may require roads, bridges, fresh water supplies, harbor renovations, orphanages, criminal work houses, a militia, etc., which, ultimately, support the general well-being of nearly all its members. The Allocation Principal does not outlaw the creation of these common goods; it merely requires that they be negotiated within the cooperative atmosphere of voluntary associations, that they persuade consent by actual necessity and not divisive compulsion, and that they be constructed with funds and labor contracted between consenting people, exclusively.

Such a limitation would greatly affect the way "common needs" are currently dealt with. Some goods would not be created that are now being planned, others would be built that would not have been otherwise. Business relationships would be forged between those who are directly affected by specific developments; businesses would be both freer and more responsive to community needs. Communities would require a great deal more active communication both within themselves and among neighboring townships; several layers of bureaucratic "middle men" would be replaced with direct involvement. There would be a great deal more money in private pockets inclined to produce necessary goods; charity would increase as the need for it would decrease. The landscape of our nation would be altered; but the alteration would be on the side of conservative progress, on the side of a dynamic which would be controlled by those most affected. In the end, a greater number of people would be involved in the decision-making processes, more people would have a greater personal stake in communal activities power would be decentralized in a healthy and energetic fashion, and greater benefits would be dispersed among a larger population.

Limitation and Structure

The Allocation Principle limits the activities of any political agent to those activities which derive their authority directly from individuals. This is the most important use of The Allocation Principle: **to limit the authority of political action by making it *allocated directly from the sovereign individual*.** This is the only system of political hierarchy which insures the universal protection of every individual's "first rights."

But limiting political action is only one step in forming a legitimate political apparatus which protects and promotes responsible pursuits of well-being. The *structure* of each limited association must be formed in such a way that legitimate limits on political action are built into their internal procedures.

Structure is suggested by social custom and pragmatism. It is usually most effective when it conserves the traditional checks and balances on coercive power that already exist in a society (e.g., Dutch town meetings, English republican delegations, African tribal confederacies, North American constitutional federalism, the capitalist-judiciary concept of contract law). It is the job of the indigenous structure employed to make political action directly accountable to the opinion and wishes of the citizenry.

It is quite possible, however, that the opinions and wishes of one portion of a citizenry will come into conflict with the "first rights" of another portion. Many laws may be asked for that actually transgress upon "first rights." The Allocation Principle, as a delimiting structural component on a constitutional level, would limit the ability of a citizenry (and the drafters and enforcers of its laws) to translate its wishes into coercive power. The Allocation Principle would cause every public and private function to be scrutinized with regard to the ethical foundation of political theory: the rights of men.

The Higher Law of "first rights" must be recognized as such. It must be more than an abstraction discussed among philosophers, a catch phrase used to arouse crowds on a campaign tour, or a defiant standard raised by an occasional martyr. "First rights" must be recognized as the fundamental Law of the Land.

SPONTANEOUS CONSONANCE

In this era of Big Government, it is difficult to imagine social mechanisms other than political institutions which protect "first rights." And yet, less planned and more spontaneous social mechanisms - such as social custom and social law, the common sense virtues of honesty and reciprocity, the complex web of associations created by free communication and commerce, the stress and demands of competitive capitalism, cooperative efforts performed voluntarily within neighborhoods and by local churches, and the "institution" of family - have contributed infinitely more to the protection of rights and the success of individual value-pursuit than any governmental apparatus ever devised. Political associations are of vital importance as the *ultimate arbitrator* of law, restitution, and criminal ostracism, but their functions and structures are built upward from the spontaneous associations and moral habits of society. Peace, prosperity, and security are mainly consequences of the natural order of communication, commerce, and custom that exists prior to governmental function. Often, these consequences cease to exist after governmental intervention.

The simple truth is that **for every social responsibility taken up by government, there is a corresponding loss of responsibility recognized by society in general (and by citizens in particular).** For those who believe in the egalitarian socialization of mankind, an increase in governmental function is sought as a solution for every social problem, real and illusory. For those who believe in equalitarian sovereignty, however, such increases are understood as the greatest threat to social consonance; they are avoided whenever possible.

The following is by no means a definitive discussion of this topic. I wish only to demonstrate the spontaneity of the most essential mechanisms which support individual advancement, rights, and value-pursuit. I use three examples: public opinion, free commerce, and family. There are many more examples, but I believe these are sufficient to put into perspective the use and limitations of political institutions.

Social Order as Common Sense

Law and order are maintained, over a period, by the consent of a majority of the citizenry, not by the force employed by political agents. Social order is a spontaneous form of societal interaction which rises upward from within a people; it is not imposed downward from without. Social law is, fundamentally, that to which a majority agrees, not that which is legislated by a minority regardless of consent. A particular social order evolves over many generations as a practical means of mutual survival and commerce. It is born from the dynamic interplay between individual necessity and general custom. It is designed by no man; rather, it is a product of the pursuit of countless individuals all seeking their own life-vision.

At its root, the stability of a society is founded on a general sense of commonality in purpose and procedure. A society's purpose (or common stake) is the protection of the well-being of its members; its most basic procedure (or social mechanism) for protecting that well-being is an indigenous sense of fairness and honesty, codified into some form of necessary reciprocity, which disciplines the harmonious commerce and communication between its self-responsible members. Without this sense of fairness and honesty, the administration of codified reciprocity breaks down, self-responsible harmony becomes impossible, and totalitarian compulsion is called in to "restabilize" the situation.

It is very easy to view government as the "keeper of the peace" since government is usually the agent which is sent out to quiet protesters, protect a country's borders, equalize criminals, etc. But the real factor in "social peace" - that is, in a vast majority of a citizenry accepting the "laws of the land" and abiding by them - is that the opinion of the vast majority either coincides or is able to conform to whatever that "law" might be. No amount of blatant force can make a people *do* things, over a period, without their consent. A government can kill dissenters, send them to "reorientation camps" and coerce them in every conceivable manner, but, in the end, governmental force cannot "keep the peace" or maintain order without the consent of the governed. Political force mixed with wide dissent is not order; it is suppressed chaos.

If order is to be "managed" in any way, it must be done by maintaining the voluntary consent of the citizenry; they must consent to abide by "the law" by choice. This involves two main forms of management: (1) duty and subservience; and (2) rational agreement. (See Rothbard's *The Ethics of Liberty*.)

(1) Duty and subservience is a form of social management that requires citizens to be servants of the will of the state. It ties virtue to obedience and makes the highest virtue the performance of one's duty to the state. Thus, a virtuous person is a citizen who does whatever the state expects of him. By doing what is "good" *voluntarily*, the individual succeeds in attaining a "state of grace" with the ruling authorities. It is, of course, nothing more than submission in the name of state-sanctioned privilege.

Duty and subservience involves manipulating a people into acquiescing to an *imposed* order. Blatant coercion may be necessary in at least the initial phases of such manipulation, but the main element is **convincing individuals of their "moral duty" to the state** and the "moral value" of self-sacrifice and subservience. This type of management requires the government to become the sole moral authority. In order to keep the peace, it defines the means and ends of human life. Consent through duty and subservience consists of liquidating individual will and restructuring it in the image of the state.

The coercion employed is continual, but not necessarily a matter of outward force. It may be a matter of education, of propaganda, of brainwashing, or merely of playing upon a "natural" combination of fear, envy, guilt, apathy, paranoia, and even altruistic devotion. But, most importantly, duty and subservience utilizes only those aspects of the human being which create dependency and selflessness. Its goal is to channel men's actions in such a way as to make them sheep, to inhibit all vestiges of true sovereignty. Blatant coercion is to be saved for actions of selfest assertion and independent judgment that come into direct conflict with the state's authority.

This form of social management puts the yoke of society onto every man's back in an effort to destroy their taste for self-responsible moral agency and their active capacity for individuality. Individual rights are everywhere superseded by the "rights of society" which, in the last analysis, become the dictates of the state.

(2) Rational agreement, on the other hand, puts great emphasis on individual judgment and selfest-interest. It demands the absence of coercion, an air of mutual respect, a tolerance of differences, and a desire to understand every viewpoint. Rational agreement recognizes the human capacity for rationality and the need for intellectual autonomy and self-ownership that is each person's birthright. Individual rights are everywhere at a premium.

Rational agreement does not seek to *impose* order; rather, it seeks an *agreement to tolerance and harmony* which, in turn, *is* order.

The fundamental argument used cannot be, "because I said so," as is the case with duty and subservience. Rather, the only argument can be, "because it is right." This sense of what is right can and will be altered in the process of rational agreement, but only slightly, and usually only in the direction of a clearer concept of what "right" is. Essentially, rational agreement is a learning process, progress on an ethical level toward more fulfilling forms of interaction. Politically, it translates into a codification of universal rights recognized by society in general. It is a recognition that rights are that which is *common* among a people.

We must not believe that, because we have learned to make laws deliberately, all laws must be deliberately made by some human agency. **Rather, a group of men can form a society capable of making laws *because they already share common beliefs* which make discussion and persuasion possible and to which the articulated rules must conform in order to be accepted as legitimate.** (F. A. Hayek, *The Constitution of Liberty*)

Rational agreement is founded on the conviction that individual men order their *own* lives; not because they follow "orders," but because they do what they think is right, and this, for the most part, is what is in their best interest. No one knows better how to live your life than you do. Thoreau put the question like this:

> Must the citizen even for a moment, or in the least degree, resign his conscience to the legislator? Why has every man a conscience, then? **I think we should be men first, subjects afterward. It is not desirable to cultivate a respect for the law, so much as for the right.** The only

obligation which I have a right to assume, is to do at any time what I think right. *(Civil Disobedience)*

When men are viewed as inherently immoral or incapable of being moral (unless forced into moral action beneath the thumb of authority), duty and subservience seems a viable means of management. When men are viewed as inherently noble, rational discourse becomes the only viable means to solve differences and generate peace.

Nearly every decision of daily life is made without respect to legislative law, but with respect to some individual "inner" law. Custom, habit, and ethics are the stuff order is made of, not court decrees and police whistles. Society has its own "inner rationality" that political institutions need not, and *should* not, interfere with, except when individual rights must be protected. Indeed, if this inner rationality is replaced by external management, the result is a continual erosion of rational independence on all fronts.

Man is fallible, to be sure, but this does not mean he must be slavishly manipulated. As Herbert Spencer observed, "The ultimate result of shielding men from the effects of their folly is to fill the world with fools."

Society and Government as Separate Entities

The major tools of society - language, pooled knowledge, currency and voluntary exchange, common behavioral expectations - evolved over ages without regard to an imposed view of utopia. None of these spontaneous tools could have been employed and perfected by a single person, or even a single generation.

Government, on the other hand, holds as its main purpose the imposition of utopian vision. Although most of the political structures employed are inherited from preceeding generations, each new generation takes up the reins of government with little regard for the past, caring only how best to remake the world. It is not surprising that most of the tools of government - armed confrontation, compulsory membership, currency manipulation, propaganda - are at odds with the more constructive tools society employs.

THE NEW AGE POLITICS

The roots of most governing bodies can be traced to war and conquest. Rulers can be traced to conquering leaders. It was not until the establishment of our own Constitutional Republic that a federal system came to power by voluntary consent. Yet even this system, because of war debts following the revolution and due to the inclinations of specific aristocratic forces inherent in colonial society, included expandable powers of tariff, taxation, eminent domain, regulation, and counterfeiting. The original constitutions which guided many of our separate states were the instruments of stratified hierarchy and inherited privilege, including broad protectionist powers and, of course, slavery. (To this day, state and local laws account for the majority of property rights violations vexing our citizenry.) Westward expansion included a chauvinistic lack of conscience, especially with regard to the Spanish, English, and American Indian, and enabled many states to be founded on military intimidation alone. And our present corporate form of statism is largely animated by the ever-increasing demands of military concerns, albeit for mostly defensive purposes. The representative nature of American government cannot be denied and must not be forgotten; but its link with hierarchy and conquest must not be overlooked.

My point is that *no* government, including our own, is a creation of some "social contract" or some other spontaneous form of voluntary association for mutual benefit. The "social contract" is a fiction. What governments actually offer a citizenry is a blank sheet which is to be "signed" *before* any specifics are worked out.

Historically, government is a creature which masters by way of intimidation, not rational persuasion or voluntary consent. What the New Age suggests is that we try to tame this creature by making it the servant instead of the master. This has been the goal of political theory since before the Magna Carta. The problem is that this taming process has resulted in a general confusing of the concepts of government and society.

Tom Paine, one of the original American theorists, knew that until the distinction between society and government was clearly understood, the nature of spontaneous social action and planned governmental action could never even be properly discussed. We must have no illusion about government, neither about its origins nor its function *in* society.

Society and Government as Separate Entities

Some writers have so confounded society with government as to leave little or no distinction between them; whereas they are not only different, but have different origins. Society is produced by our wants, and government by our wickedness; the former promotes our happiness *positively* by uniting our affections, the latter *negatively* by restraining our vices. The one encourages intercourse, the other creates distinctions. The first is patron, the last a punisher.

Society in every state is a blessing, but Government, even in its best state, is but a necessary evil, in its worst state an intolerable one... Government, like dress, is the badge of lost innocence; the palaces of kings are built on the ruins of the bowers of paradise.

Here then is the origin of government; namely, a mode rendered necessary by the inability of moral virtue to govern the world. (*Common Sense*)

A grave mistake is made if this "mode" made necessary by our own moral inadequacies is allocated the moral authority to remake the world in its own image. It is in the nature of modern government to disguise its coercive mechanisms as virtue incarnate, its decrees as moral absolutes, and its goals as consentaneous with society's. But modern government seeks to perpetuate its static self at the expense of the dynamic social consonance. It desires order for the purpose of administrative ease, not primarily for the administration of justice. It uses force in the protection of its own position of privilege, not exclusively in the protection of personal sovereignty. Too often government is, in every active phase, demonstratibly callous, bullying, and opposed to society's best interests.

Legitimate political associations must be generated from within society as one more aspect of social order. They are to correct the basic social evil: the destruction or threat of destruction of one's values by another. They must *not* impose their own brand of destruction or create their own species of chaos.

Society and government must always be recognized as separate, else government will claim itself as not only one guardian of individual rights among many, but the exclusive originator of all rights. When that happens, "individual rights" will no longer exist (except as Orwellian newspeak). Governmental privilege and prerogative will have replaced them.

"Society as Criminal" Creates Need for Political Action

The need for federalized political associations does not arise merely because a certain small percentage of a society is crooked. Individual criminals could be handled by police and local courts based on a generally accepted social law. It is a bigger and more basic problem which brings on the need for large scale political action.

Of course, there is the threat of massive foreign conquest. The need to mobilize in some cooperative manner to protect national boarders suggests, at the very least, an appropriately fashioned confederacy which could contribute in concert to self-defense. But political associations are also meant to protect the individual from conquering forces within his own society: slavery, exploitation, abject conformity. When *society in general* becomes a criminal by demanding submission to hierarchical "social duties" or coercive "social leaders," political action must defend the individual's rightful self-ownership. This is what Rand meant when she stated that rights protect the individual from "the altruistic demands of society." Political institutions must set themselves between the individual and society in order to protect that individual in the face of overbearing societal demands of stratified subservience and collective desire.

The only long-term, constructive deterrent to societal criminality is the equalitarian concept of legal rights backed by protective political force. . . and the philosophical knowledge that (1) rights find there source in the *individual*, not society, and (2) legitimate political force is an intrument of universal *individual* rights, not collective caprice.

Society as Criminal Creates Need for Political Action

> Whether the rights of men shall be equal is not a matter of opinion but of right, and consequently of principle; for men do not hold their rights as a grant from each other, but each one in right of himself. (Tom Paine, *Dissertation on First Principle of Government*)

Society, as a whole, does not usually embrace the concept of individual rights. On the contrary, violence against the individual nearly always takes on the righteous posture of being in "society's best interest." Couple this posture with the view that government is the right hand of the social will, and you have the dilemma of democratic man.

> A lot of us want something-for-nothing, or at least something-for-less, and so we create the State in our own image. Only a moral transformation will change that image, and nothing short of this will topple the State. **A people with larceny in their souls will eventually write it into their statutes, as we have done.** If people covet their neighbor's property they will find legal ways to get their hands on it, and a pliant "social conscience" will bend around to approve. (Edmund A. Opitz, from the Introduction to Nock's *Our Enemy, The State*)

Our own history clearly shows that once the public no longer strongly supports the principles of inviolate individual rights, government will be quick to aid them in any transgressions they may desire. Every anecdotal failure of free commerce, every poor man's need, every rich man's desire, every prophet's vision will constitute another cause to inflate the State's powers of confiscation, conscription, and counterfeiting.

Where, then, does that leave us?. Is the individual hopelessly crushed between the collectivist insticts of society and the ravenous powers of political expansionism?

Remember that the local checks and balances of republican government failed to save the Negro from the coercive social system of slavery. And yet emancipation occured. Even after the Civil War, generations continued under immense social exploitation. And yet the civil rights movement shook our nation like a mighty storm. In many ways, government was dragged along, kicking and screaming in protest, not wanting to change the status quo. In other ways, it played an aggressive, constructive role. One would not be overstating the case to admit that social progress might not have been possible without its protective intervention.

But it wasn't government *per se* that made it all happen; it was the public's perception that people were being wronged, that human dignity was being attacked, that rights were being denied. Without this extra-political moral sense, progress in the name of the individual would never have occured.

No progress is possible unless a sufficient number of people want it. The battle for freedom cannot be removed from this level, from the level of wants, of moral support, of public action in the name of individual rights.

Free Trade: Commerce as Needs Satisfaction

There is another extra-political force which supports the concept of individual rights: free trade.

Free trade is not an instrument of utopian vision. It disdains coercion, distrusts privilege, and ignores hierarchy. In fact, free trade is simply *a voluntary system of satisfying needs*.

Within the context of capitalistic commerce, one person's product is meant, for the most part, to satisfy another person's need. To produce a good or service which satisfies a need is to provide something of value to someone else. That someone else, the buyer of the good, provides something of value to the seller in return. A trade is made that benefits both parties and satisfies independently determined needs. It is need that, for the most part, creates value in the free market.

Other systems of social order attempt to satisfy needs as well. But only free trade enables an individual to identify his own needs and to make sure he himself is satisfied. All other systems employ an authority which determines who satisfies whose needs and what those needs are. All other systems attempt to satisfy needs outside the context of legitimate rights, outside the concept of the individual.

Free and dynamic commerce "structures" society along the lines of mutually beneficial associations. An entrepreneur puts up a shop where there is a demand for it or where it is convenient for him. A laborer provides his services where there is a demand for them within the limits of his own need and/or convenience. People are free to structure their own lives to fulfill their own distinct needs and to satisfy other people's distinct needs. Lines of communication and trade are opened along lines of necessity and interest.

Like an expanding wall covered with years of overlapping, smudged, sometimes brilliantly vibrant graffiti, this dynamic structure is never really unified, never competely balanced, and eternally riddled with mistakes, unsatisfied desires, and a little pornography. But consentaneous commerce will establish better than any other system a streamlined means of large scale needs satisfaction. The fact that the free market places the responsibility on each individual to utilize his own situation to his best advantage is what forces the structure to fit the needs of those who use it. Over a period, voluntary exchange will become more efficient than any other system at satisfying needs because satisfying needs is its sole purpose.

Capitalism is often condemned because its only purpose is supposedly the accumulation of capital. Large amounts of capital enables commerce to be carried out on the institutional scale of corporations, which, in turn, makes for the even larger accumulation of capital as these corporations merge. The fear is that monopolies result, or at least a corporate aristocracy that is able to demolish its competition with relentless pricing deals and trade manipulation. This would be a danger to the necessary dispersal of property and dynamic pluralism within a society and would seriously threaten the energy and health that society might otherwise achieve.

But the capital accumulations of large corporations carries a heavy burden: they must take the long view, the conservative path that leads to steady growth and balanced pricing. This capital accumulation also gives them the freedom to explore, among other things, new possibilities in highly technichal fields of research. In addition, free commerce includes competitive and cooperative enterprises on a smaller scale which interweave into a strong and innovative, yet essentially decentralized, "organic unit." This "unit" is able to compete with centralized corporations both in terms of pricing and less definable human fulfillment. While producing one aspect of the "unit's" end product, these small operations are still very connected to the community in which they reside, yet remain uniquely sensitive to the market demands in which they gain profit. This system of big *and* small enables both resiliency and stabilty to be achieved, both independent innovation and long-term capital intensive research to continue, and is able to interconnect tiny communities around the world both directly or through the seasoned hand of international corporations.

(It should be noted that the goal of *all* socio-economic systems is to "accumulate capital." The real difference between what has been specifically termed "capitalism" and other economic systems is that coercive force is to be outlawed within the "structure" of the free market, whereas coercive force is the central aspect of other authority-dominated politically controlled markets.)

No other structure can act so quickly to meet new aspirations, since no other structure is as directly tied to individual needs, interests, and abilities. No other structure enables such a fast and honest flow of information to move from person to person, since no other structure lets individuals determine what they need and lets them free to satisfy that need. No other structure provides the same amount of innovation, since no other system lets goods and knowledge be judged on success and individual interest (as opposed to orthodoxy or some centrally controlled estimate of "utility"). And no other system keeps prices (the monetary value of goods) free from interference so to keep them a true gauge of supply and demand.

At the heart of the free market is one impersonal test: *effectiveness.* An individual is judged, ideally, only on his ability to effect a desired result. He is not judged by his skin color, his political opinions, his religion. You probably do not know if the chair you are sitting on was made by a woman or man, an atheist or Moslem, a bigot or pacifist. You know only that, if it is well made, it was made by someone who valued fine workmanship; if it was mass produced, it satisfies your needs within your particular budget. This impersonal test of effectiveness replaces other tests which have determined the system of trade up until modern times: bloodline, class, guild, party status, or some other form of collective elitism. Capitalism recognizes only effectiveness; it does not discriminate. In fact, discrimination is viewed with contempt since it inhibits free exchange and economic progress.

Not only does the free market help protect an individual against discrimination, it increases an individual's capacity for intellectual independence. You are more able to be independent in every way if you are free to make your own associations and pursue unregulated knowledge in a voluntary market. Neither the state nor the rich have a monopoly on such things as scientific facts, the arts, education, morality, recreation, etc. If you are free from coercion and able to obtain enough wealth to satisfy your need for survival, then all other endeavors can be toward any purpose you yourself decide (within and because of the universal limits of "first rights"). Your intellectual life is your own, absolutely.

And, related to this idea, you are free to pass on to your family any surplus wealth you may have accrued (or to anyone else you so choose). In this way, the common desire to make life more secure and joy more attainable for loved ones can be realized by simply extending the principles of property rights to include all aspects of the free market. The values of family and loved ones are enhanced by a secure structure of voluntary association and property rights, enhanced because they are protected from abuse and interference.

All this is possible without the aid of an imposed, centralized structure. In fact, there is a great deal of evidence to suggest that it would not be possible if order was centrally imposed instead of spontaneously developed. In an imposed order prices no longer reflect true market conditions, people make judgments on false information, property rights are infringed, privilege is reinstated, associations are no longer due to mutual benefit, individuals no longer control their own lives.

The free market is made possible by the existence of property rights, contract law, identifiable and sound currency, and a sufficient dispersal of property among an honest, ambitious people. Where political action is needed to protect these prerequisites, it is a partner to the free market; but it must never inhibit the market's spontaneity or destroy or assault any of the necessary conditions for the market's survival.

Most people who crusade against freedom believe that order can be achieved only by the rule of one person over another, by the majority being guided by some "commanding intelligence." Modern economic theory has shown, through an analysis of actual economic activity and the theoretical works of men from Adam Smith to Ludwig von Mises, that spontaneous order can be achieved in a free market. Free trade "creates" a structure based on "the mechanisms of mutual adjustments by individuals." This is "order without command" (Hayek).

The free market, above all, is a system of commerce between people devoid of compulsion and coercion in its many violent and subtle manifestations. It is the ultimately *human* form of rational and voluntary interaction based on mutual respect, a recognition of individual dignity, and a commitment to peaceful exchange.

Needs Satisfaction vs. Legislative Mandates

There are many examples of whole industries which have grown and expanded - because of need - in the free market, industries which government could never have thought of, or, if they had, could never manage with near the efficiency. The reason is that **governmental functions are not tied to entrepreneurial success (the ability to actually satisfy needs), but only to political success (the ability to satisfy legislative mandates).** In the free market, needs are defined by the needy; in political institutions, needs are defined by legislators and the mechanics of bureaucratic structure. (See Ludwig von Mises' *Socialism* and *Human Action*.)

Profits occur when the cost to satisfy a need is less than the value placed on that satisfaction by the "needer" (the buyer). Profit-making is the ability to satisfy needs at a cost which is sufficiently beneath the value attached to that satisfaction by the prospective needer. The producer of the satisfaction attempts to make his production design more efficient so to decrease his own costs and increase his profits. To do so is to satisfy a need with less waste and less delay.

When viewed in this manner, economic efficiency is seen as a highly ethical goal.

One example of an industry that provides the satisfaction of needs often thought of as belonging to the political domain is the insurance industry. Insurance covers everything from death to hospital costs to damage to property to capital investments. In fact, wherever there is a risk of any kind, insurance can cover that risk, and at quite reasonable rates. Consider what the insurance industry would be like today - in terms of responsiveness, rates, and areas of coverage - if the federal government would have nationalized it fifty years ago (instead of merely regulating it to near stagnation)? Worse yet, what if government would have understood insurance as one of its constitutional functions two hundred years ago, the industry as we know it today would not even exist.

Many modern governmental functions, in one way or another, come under the "insurance" heading. Unemployment compensation, worker's (disability) compensation, social security, and medicare are a few examples. We see their costs rising dramatically and inflation in the fields they are meant to serve. We see the programs expanded to include functions that have nothing to do with the insurance aspect, bloating their budgets beyond what is necessary, hurting those who need the essential services that were first provided. We see deficits, bureaucratic waste and fraud, mismanagement, delays in claims, files lost or completely mixed up, and an increased capacity for abuse by claimants due to inadequate surveillance. We see little competition in these fields because of the monopolistic forces which the government exerts whenever it intervenes in the market: no recourse to governmental decisions, no alternative services, a leveling of services to a lowest common denominator, the inability of programs to progress or change with changing needs, inefficiency - all these problems create further problems that are then dealt with by imposing more regulations and increasing taxes. The cycle, over the long-term, can grow only more oppressive and inefficient.

Within the private sector, the insurance industry meets these same needs and makes a profit at the same time. They meet these needs *because* they are a profit-seeking industry. Profit-making is efficiency, and efficiency is meeting needs as quickly and cheaply as possible.

I do not mean to defend every aspect of the insurance industry. I do not mean to indicate that insurance rates are exceptionally low or that their corporate functioning is exceptionally efficient. (I would consider the heavy regulatory interference that they must contend with from governmental agencies before casting any stones.) My point here is that, in general, the free market can meet almost any kind of need. And it can meet needs so much better when left unfettered by regulation and monopolistic intervention. If it were truly nationalized, the insurance industry would be in much worse shape. If deregulated, it would be in much better shape. It is one example of private enterprise doing its job: satisfying needs in a context of mutually beneficial voluntary exchanges.

Now, consider the area of charity. Within the bureaucratic Welfare State, 60% of all revenue assigned to charity goes toward operating costs. Private sector figures are under 20% (many are below 10%). Plus, the majority of welfare funds that make it beyond the pockets of government workers go toward middle or upper income recepients in the form of social security which augments private retirement plans, unemployment payments for seasonal workers, direct subsidies, etc. The vast majority of private sector charity, however, goes directly to the needy or appropriate research institutions.

It seems the private sector wins in both the profit and nonprofit fields.

The problem with capitalism is that efficiency *in general* can still mean a lack of success at meeting needs *in particular*. The poor and uninformed all too easily "miss out" on the efficient programs provided by a specific free market industry. But, historically, this is usually only a short-term problem. Once the specific industry expands, once its capital increases, once it learns to better manage its resources, the costs for its services or goods comes down. More people will then be able to utilize that industry. In the long-term, services and goods that were at first only for the rich become available for everyone else. (Witness: telephones, radios, appliances, housing, clothing, education, the use of lawyers, computerized services.) This is so because new services and goods are risky and/or limited, and, thus, expensive. They become less risky and less limited only through productive efficiency and an increase in production capabilities. It is only when long-term progress is retarded by intervention (regulation, taxes, government protected monopolies, etc.) that this process ceases. If an industry is forced to service those who cannot meet the cost of production, then future growth is impeded, research and experimentation into new techniques is distorted or prolonged or dropped altogether, and the ability to meet new needs and new demands is damaged. All economic activities take excessive capital (sufficient profits) and incentive based on real market information. They do not come about because the state demands it. Innovation and entrepreneurial courage cannot be legislated.

It is easy for one who is not poor to have the patience to wait for an industry to expand sufficiently so that it can include the poorer members of society. It is not so easy for the poor. What must also be considered is that the free market enables the poor and uninformed to benefit from innovations and increased wealth more quickly and completely (and more *permanently*) than any other economic system. The free market is able to create more wealth faster than any other mechanism. The advent of free market mass production has brought everything from books to gourmet coffee blends to every man's fingertips. Scientific and manufacturing advancements in farming and industry have brought or kept prices down for nearly every product, especially essentials like food and clothing, while disseminating those products throughout society faster than ever before. An individual need know nothing about production, he does not have to have an ounce of ambition, he may be unlucky enough to be born in a Chicago ghetto, and he still can benefit from these aspects of the free market. But if he does have ambition, he is protected by equalitarian property rights in any productive endeavor.

Instead of asking government to intervene in the egalitarian leveling of economic prosperity, it should be asked: What is keeping prosperity from reaching the broadest base possible? For example, why has the work week remained at 40 hours per week for the past five decades while capital investment and productivity have grown at unprecedented rates? Why do increasingly large numbers of families have to have both parents working to maintain a slipping standard of living? Why has the optimism of the last 100 years, that children would grow up in a more prosperous world than their parents, been replaced with the opposite expectation? Why hasn't government been implicated in these great scandals?

It is estimated that the United States would have eight times the spendable income we now have if not for the direct and indirect costs of government intervention. (See Neil Smith's *The Probability Broach*). That translates into a five hour work week to maintain our current standard of living. Imagine what a 36 hour work week would maintain.

Imagine our society if its wealth were increased by a factor of two or four or eight. Wouldn't more people be covered by insurances? Wouldn't there be greater participation in essential industries? Wouldn't there be industries we can't even imagine today? Wouldn't there be far less poverty? More opportunity? This would have been the case if government had never intervened in the market - except to protect property rights and their antecedant "first rights." This would have been the case if all industries - banking, investments, production, communications, utilities, etc. - had been protected by law only to ensure life and liberty, instead of regulated, reorganized, and centralized for the benefit of legislators, unions, frightened producers, millionaire owners, and the status quo. This would have been the case if taxes had not been stripped from society, if that wealth had been translated instead into decentralized capital investments, innovative and productive industry, and used to generate new wealth and new, thus far unimagined, products and services.

This same reasoning applies to the future. What will it be like if we continue to let government intervene in the workings of society through incredibly high tax rates, incredibly oppressive regulations, and by protecting and reorganizing whole industries and services with monopolistic sanctions? What could it be like if we do not? What would our lives be like if they were really free, instead of regulated by legislative whim? What might happen if we were protected from intervention of every kind, instead of ordered to live within a general state of mutual intervention? We cannot know the answers to these questions. But our educated guesses should be sufficient to demand freedom for our lives, our minds, our personal associations, and our markets. Not just our prosperity hinges upon such a decision, but our capacity to achieve well-being as well.

The Family

All formal associations of people within society form a kind of institution, after they have grown big enough and been around long enough. Regardless of what traditions and bureaucratic codes might develop, free associations are usually intended to serve the individual in his quest for comfort, satisfaction, and self-expansion. That this equation is often turned around - so that the individual is made to serve the institution - is one of the major problems of modern times.

The danger of turning the self-making equation around is also present with regard to the most basic of all social groupings: the family. The family is a social unit whose members do not all come together voluntarily. Husband and wife come together out of their own volition, in our modern culture, but children certainly are not voluntary members, at least not originally. And they are bound by forces greater than comfort and pleasure and curiosity. Family members are bound by the needs of human survival, intense emotional bonds, shared physical characteristics and habits and psychological traits. These forces can serve to enslave an individual through guilt and psychological dependency. But they more often provide a steady framework in which an individual grows to maturity and independence. In fact, the bonds of family are potentially the most supportive and sustaining of any which occur during a person's lifetime.

The family serves the great purpose of providing a means of survival on not only a "material" level, but also by nurturing an individual with love and security. An infant is more than a machine which must be fed and changed; it is a growing being which requires compassion, which needs warmth, which must be held and loved and cherished. Its needs must be understood and met with a special quality of caring and purpose. This is what makes for a secure and happy beginning in life. And it is the basis for all intellectual endeavors which occur in the many years to come. This is the essential purpose of the family.

The family is a natural and spontaneous outgrowth of man's nature and man's needs. It is the first association in the hierarchy of groupings concerned with the survival and education of the individual. And it is, in general, the most influential "institution" with regard to an individual's personality, sense of self and life, and his life-habits which assist or inhibit his ability to attain joy and fulfillment and personal success.

For the most part, no one is more aware of a child's needs and styles of learning and living than that child's parents. No one is more concerned about that child's authentic well-being. This is why the family is not merely one more example of a spontaneous structure in society. It is of primary importance because of its unique position and power in the development of the individual.

People who are sensitive to this fact are very protective of their family privacy, their family cohesiveness, their family interdependencies. In other words, they are very *possessive* of their families. Why is this? They believe they *know best* what the individual members of their family need, what their aspirations are, and how fragile their quests might be. They believe their family members have a right to pursue the kind of life style that they derive from those needs and aspirations and that they should be protected from transgressions which delimit their personal quests. They believe that the private sphere of self-possession and self-power includes themselves, their household, and their children.

I agree. The laws of an ethical society must protect the private sphere of family from any coercive intervention from outsiders. How can this be done? The best answer lies in the concept of *trusteeship*.

The Concept of Trusteeship. Children, like any other human being, are self-owned. They cannot be anyone's property, including their parents'. But they must be under the guardianship of someone until they are able to exercise the qualities of independence which include the capacity to "make their own way" - either by their own labor or in concert with other-than-family partners. Until that time, they require help - a guardian who looks after their long-term welfare. The concept of family guardianship could be stated: the parent is the guardian of a child's welfare until the child attains the capacity to look after its own welfare independent of its parents.

Normally, a child's first guardians are its biological mother and father. In a two parent situation, both parents retain joint guardianship. If, however, the biological father is not known or does not assume the responsibilities of guardianship, the mother would have an undivided guardianship. This would be the case regardless of the marital status of the parents. Family is, first, a biological concept. It cannot be dictated by legislative law or religious convention. The biological parents are the initial guardians unless they transfer their guardianship to others or abuse it in some dramatic fashion that requires intervention for the protection of the child.

The problem is that the concept of guardianship is not specifically defined within the general context of "first rights." To remain consistent within a legal framework of property rights, guardianship must be made a property right of the guardian. This is the concept of trusteeship.

A trustee is the legal guardian of an individual. A trusteeship is property unto itself in that it gives title to the owner to specific rights regarding the individual in question. These rights include the right to look after the welfare of the individual in question. They include the rights of protection: no one has the authority to usurp the powers of guardianship unless the trustee should abuse her/his duties as a trustee. In this manner, the private sphere of family is protected by the same legal sanctions and ethical authority as the private sphere of self and property.

It is this *trusteeship* that the parent(s) owns, not the child itself. And it is this trusteeship that becomes endowed with the right of use and disposal, not the child.

A parent retains property rights to his/her child's trusteeship as long as that child requires parental care. During that time, neither the state, nor any other institution, can abridge that right. Neither can the parent abuse the child in any manner. Trusteeship is defined as: the guardianship of a designated dependent's welfare. If a parent does not perform the duties of a trustee, she/he can be legally stripped of this property right.

What a political agent has authority to do is provide for the self-defense of children and spouses and parents. Political action can provide protection for their body, property, and psychological well-being. It cannot, however, dictate to a legitimate trustee (the parent) what should be done with a child and how to accomplish that end. It can only legislate what is an infringement of the individual's rights and then protect the individual against infringement and try to collect restitution when an infringement occurs. The child is protected from violence by its own "first rights" and the family is protected from coercive interference and arbitrary transgressions by the property rights of trusteeship.

Such a property rights approach to trusteeship would greatly simplify family law. It would also simplify the issues regarding what rights parents have in choosing activities for their children (schooling, recreational activities, religious upbringing, etc.) Unless the trustee can be proven as abusing her/his trusteeship, the trustee retains the rights of choice and style within the private sphere of family action. It protects the family from outside interference by defining parenthood (trusteeship) in the context of property rights.

The reason for doing this is plain: the family, as a private institution founded on the protection and maintenance of individual well-being, is a vital element in an individual's life-making process. It must be legally recognized and protected in a manner consistent with individual rights protection. The concept of trusteeship accomplishes this goal.

Enforceable trusteeship also protects children by tying the concept of parenting to a legal contractual concept, making their own rights of self-ownership and freedom from coercion easier to defend and easier to administer. And, once the adolescent-adult can show that he/she no longer requires a trustee (regardless of any arbitrary age), he/she is backed by the powers of justice if he/she desires to pursue his/her own separate life.

Parenting can be the most totalitarian of positions in society; childhood the most slavish. It has been pointed out by Dr. Peter Breggin (*The Psychology of Freedom*) that child abuse has one primary cause: the parent has total control over a child's life and, unless severe scars result, is answerable to no one for her/his parenting methods. Where totalitarian powers exist, abuse resides.

The child must be protected from abuse by having the outlet to leave his/her home environment freely and sue for either a transfer of trusteeship or legal independence. This not only includes the physical and emotional abuse of violent parents, but the intellectual abuse caused by the aberrant parent who would, in a freer society, keep their children from all educational experiences or force them into anti-educational schools which teach only ignorance, intolerance, and ignobility. Law is to protect the "must" actions required in pursuing one's well-being. A trustee must not only be kept from outright aggression against these "must" actions (locking a child in a closet without food), but from passively circumventing them as well (starving an infant by neglect or exposure). The trustee, under this law, must attempt to nurture the entire mix of characteristics which support maturity and indepenence. Failure to do so should be met with protective intervention, community-based counsel, and, finally, a withdrawal of trusteeship.

I realize that I have not set down specific guidelines for what is legitimate trusteeship. Any discussion of it would more or less coincide with common sense. I only wish to point out that the family is a very important spontaneous institution which aids an individual's survival and over-all ability to gain independence and self-control. It must be afforded its own private sphere within the coherent concept of rights else the State will have the power to intervene with the same vigor it displays when controlling the market "for the good of all."

Property Rights and the Transfer of Trusteeship. There is another consequence to the property rights concept of trusteeship. In the course of looking after her/his own welfare as well as her/his child's, a trustee would be able to pass on her/his trusteeship to another individual or agency. In other words, a trustee could sell her/his trusteeship, trade it in a voluntary exchange, or transfer the rights of trusteeship in any manner which would be acceptable to the child's long-term welfare. Such a transfer would probably happen only when the parent could not handle the responsibilities of parenthood due to economic conditions, age, health, emotional stability, or possible incompatibility with the child. But if such an option were exercised, the trustee (and not an adoption agency) would set the terms of any exchange as the legitimate *owner* of the rights to trusteeship.

The practical effect of such a policy is that the trustee (for example, a single mother living in poverty or an unwed teenager) cannot become a victim in any adoption scheme. The trustee is protected aginst fraud, misrepresentation, manipulation, extortion, etc., just like any other entrepreneur. She/he cannot be strong-armed into "giving up" the child because of economic circumstances or social status. She/he cannot be forced to use an adoption service that keeps the names of future guardians a secret. Also, she would be able to obtain compensation for her loss. (Presently, only the adoption agency is able to benefit from such an exchange.)

A voluntary exchange of trusteeship would circumvent the highly discriminatory concept of "fitness" which often disqualifies poor and minority individuals. Questions of fitness would be determined by the trustee (the person who is, in general, most attached to the child). The only standard would be a child's long-term welfare, not the size of a couple's income or their social standing. In addition, far more options would be open to each trustee: whether to transfer or sell the rights of trusteeship to a neighbor, a relative, a known family, a family whose identity is secret, what visitation rights can be negotiated with the receiving party, etc. Within the concept of trusteeship, the parent is better able to personally look after the future welfare of her/his child.

No human being can be sold into slavery. This is a direct consequence of "first rights." Neither should any individual be abused in any manner. This is true for infants as well as adults. Selling or transfering the rights of trusteeship is not a form of slave trading. It is merely a form of exercising one's obligations to one's children in a context of voluntary association and mutual benefit. It involves all interested parties, not just the interests of the obtaining party or the intermediate agency.

The beauty and importance of family must be protected. It must be protected from any intervention which would destroy its capacity to nurture the individual toward independence. It is one more example which shows the importance of rights in limiting interference and coercion.

THE PROPER ATTRIBUTES OF POLITICAL ASSOCIATIONS

I do not intend to debate the virtues of one specific style of limited government over another. Such debate would have to include a complex analysis of the specific culture in question, analysis which is beyond the scope of this book. I intend instead to center on the general attributes of political power and function which enable political associations to perform their single task of "first rights" protection while keeping them from expanding on or abusing that task.

The following is a summary of the eight most important attributes of legitimate government.

The Allocation Principle and Rights Protection

In practical terms, the function of government is one of protecting people and property. This has been the belief of libertarian-conservative theorists since the Enlightenment:

> The commonwealth seems to be a society of men constituted only for the procuring, preserving, and advancing of their own civil interests.
>
> Civil interests I call life, liberty, health, and indolency of body; and the possession of outward things, such as money, lands, houses, furnitures and the like.
>
> The political society is instituted for no other end, but to secure every man's possession of the things of this life. The care of each man's soul and the things of heaven, which neither does belong to the commonwealth nor can be subject to it, is left entirely to every man's self. (John Locke, *Letter Concerning Tolerance*)

By securing the right to legitimate possessions, the right to ethical pursuits is secured. The government, by being banned from meddling in ethical pursuits, becomes a protector of ethical pursuits, for it insulates each individual in his determination of means and ends (within the concept of rights protection). In addition, by being banned from economic intervention, government becomes a protector of economic prosperity, for it insulates productive associations from violence, theft, fraud, and unnatural instability, without inducing its own disincentives and distortions. Force is to be used exclusively to protect the individual's justified liberties. It is a very simple concept, but a very difficult one for government to accept.

With this in mind, the most comprehensive act of any American reformer would be to amend the U. S. Constitution with the delimiting demands of The Allocation Principle. By affixing The Allocation Principle to the ultimate law of the land, all political action, for the first time in the history of this nation, would be judged relative to the most equalitarian and noncoercive of standards: individual rights.

Isonomy: Equality of Law

Isonomy is a term that is currently obsolete, no longer used in our language today (although the term "equalitarian," which I have used above, is beginning to take hold). Isonomy was employed by the Greeks as *isonomia: isos* meaning equal, and *nomos* meaning distribution of spontaneous law and custom. Isonomy was used by early Enlightenment writers to signify the concept of "equality of law." It meant that law should pertain equally to all men, that the distribution of law is universal and that the source of law is the needs of men which spontaneously arise in the course of voluntary interaction. Justice is blind: all men are the same before her. Law is natural: it protects the natural pursuits of the individual from unexpected aggression and undesired interference. It is indeed an out-of-date concept in this age of discretionary powers, judicial relativism, and democratic mandates. The time has come to resurrect it.

Isonomy negates the possibility of privilege and exception. If all citizens - lawmaker, law enforcer, and law abider - are equal before the law, if all laws pertain to all men, absolutely, then no one can be granted a privilege before the law and no exception can be made beneath the law. Isonomy does not necessarily mean that people will be free or even adequately protected against transgressions. But it does mean that no privilege can exist within the state apparatus or beneath state power. Arbitrary state compulsion is, therefore, highly unlikely since such compulsion would apply to the lawmakers as well as the rest of the citizenry. State power is thus limited by the human desire for *self*-power which, for the most part, exists in lawmakers and law abiders alike.

The possibility exists that a society would want all members equally oppressed, as opposed to equally free. This is the case in countries such as the Islamic Republic of Iran. There, religious intolerance and anti-individualistic commandments create societal demands ranging from general subservience to masochistic, self-annihilating activities. Isonomy will not aid in limiting the power of a state in such a society. But in most of the Western world where spontaneous social law and custom includes attitudes of respect for true personal sovereignty, where rational and constructive individualism still has great personal appeal, isonomy is a powerful ally of liberty. It is a concept which disallows discrimination, monopoly and guild power, and extends no special sanctions to the status quo.

Isonomy, when linked to the concept of "first rights," helps to limit the state's capacity for coercive action. By making law equal for every single individual, the idea of "rule" is more closely identified with the concept of "enforcing general rules laid down irrespective of the particular case and equally applicable to all," as opposed to the concept of "making one man obey another man's will" (Hayek).

Isonomy, alone, is not the cornerstone of political theory. But it is vital in retaining the legitimacy of political authority, in limiting a government's capacity for coercion, and in protecting the free market from monopolistic or anti-competitive intervention. If isonomy is not an element of political power, rulers become a privileged class unto themselves, those with the best state contacts profit at the expense of everyone else, and the state becomes an apparatus of elitism and parasitism.

In the modern world where the concept of isonomy is obsolete, this is indeed the case.

Predictability

> [If we wish to] establish [a social order] where intelligent human beings use their individual capacities as successfully as possible in their pursuit of their own ends, the chief requirement for its establishment is that each know which of the circumstances in his environment he can count on... [The] protection against unpredictable interference... is the essential condition of individual freedom, and to secure it is the main function of law. (Hayek, *The Constitution of Liberty*)

This implies two kinds of predictability: (1) predictability with respect to social interaction, and (2) predictability with respect to political action. This predictability can be analyzed as a freedom from two kinds of arbitrary and unforseeable action: (1) freedom from the sudden and arbitrary aggressions of private individuals and associations, and (2) freedom from the undefined or arbitrary actions of government.

(1) To promote predictability, law must protect the individual and his property. This protects people from bodily harm and coercion. Property rights are upheld; contract rights are honored; commerce continues in a context of protected freedom. In this manner, individuals can plan their own lives in a high degree of certainty, interrupted only by the occassional surprises nature supplies. A great deal of predictability is achieved, and people profit from it by way of personal freedom, collective security, and gratifying stability.

(2) To promote predictablity, law must be generally applied to all individuals (so that privilege does not become a matter of unpredictable legislative whim) and it must be specific and comprehensible in its interpretation (so that it can be understood and duely planned for by both the individual and the courts). Law must be like any other aspect of predictable reality: it must be a "fixed feature" in one's environment that one can rationally cope with. If law *prohibits* specific actions but refrains from *mandating* any action, and if it is applied to everyone in the same manner regardless of circumstances, then individuals will be protected from potentially undefined and arbitrary state coercion.

If these two features of law remain intact, an individual can gain a high degree of confidence in intelligent action that would otherwise be impossible. He can also retain self-respect while remaining a law-abiding citizen, for he can act for his own self-interest and at the same time avoid breaking any of the laws of the land.

This suggests a third aspect of predictability: limiting the number of laws to a manageable amount. As James Madison cautioned:

> It will be of little avail to the people that the laws are made by men of their own choice, if the laws are so voluminous that they cannot be read, or so incoherent that they cannot be understood; if they be repealed or revised before they are promulgated, or undergo such incessant changes that no man, who knows what the law is today, can guess what it will be like tomorrow.

Of course, predictability by itself does not make a law good. It just makes breaking it more avoidable. But the price paid for ignoring predictability is heavy: capriciousness in government, instability in the marketplace, businesses taking the short-term view (since the long-term would include too many political variables), envy and apathy among the citizenry, and even psychological neurosis due to perennial uncertainty. The price of unpredictability is, essentially, a lack of ethical rationality and creative energy within individual people. Energy can only be made constructive when people are able to plan their futures within a stable and knowable environment. Rationality exists as a social context only when people are able to exercise their responsibility-in-freedom without the threat of violence or manipulation.

Without predictability, society crumbles. Although government will try to reimpose order through additional interventions, only further chaos will result. If predictability is lacking, no amount of statist glue can hold a people together.

No Monopoly Powers

As a consequence of isonomy, government would be unable to grant monopoly status to any agent, class, business, or industry. This would be a blatant form of inequality before the law.

Monopoly status is governmental sanction. It is a statist protection against competition which is extended as a privilege to an individual, agency, or corporation. It is not merely an agent or corporation obtaining a "corner on the market" and thus becoming a dominant influence in that particular field. Monopoly status means that someone or some group has "exclusive control of a commodity or service in a given market; an exclusive privilege of engaging in or providing a particular service, granted by a ruler or the state" (*Webster's Unabridged Dictionary*). In a pluralistic society where property is dispersed among individuals, a monopoly can only be achieved and sustained, over a period, by governmental sanction. When voluntary association and property rights are everywhere upheld, exclusion from any noncoercive activity is forbidden by law, competition is always possible, and "exclusive privilege" impossible.

The most popular argument for monopolies is embodied in the "natural monopoly" theory: Certain services necessary to a community do not produce a profit, let alone support competition, and, in most instances, would never even be performed at all without governmental assistance (such as the mass diversion of fresh water from rivers and lakes to major metropolitan areas and the construction of centralized nuclear power plants); these services must either be paid for by tax dollars or protected from risk with price supports, monopoly status, and manditory consumption within the community. The "natural monopoly" theory usually coexists with the notion that "natural" resources like drinkable water and electric power are common property to be shared by every citizen *by right*. The result is that resources are underpriced, overconsumed, and badly managed. The biggest winners are the "natural monopolies" themselves.

Even if a certain "necessary" service required public assistance to be initiated, is it government's place to determine if competition is feasible once the service has been established? Does it have the right to keep entrepreneurs from attempting to break into these fields? Does it have the right to predetermine where consumers go for specific services or commodities? If so, from where does it derive such authority?

Clearly, The Allocation Principle can be invoked to show that no individual has the right to keep another from noncoercive entrepreneurship or voluntary exchange; thus, government (the people's agent) has no legitimate claim to such a power.

The same argument disgraces the monopoly status granted to licensed professionals. There is no question that, especially within a free market society, licensing by professional associations and educational institutions would greatly enhance an entrepreneur's prestige and respectability. It would undoubtedly make procuring insurance easier. But that the state must limit access to specific markets to state-certified individuals is clearly a case of illegitimate privilege. That a person is or is not state-certified hardly determines if he or she would be a knowledgeable and effective teacher, lawyer, accountant, utility supplier, social worker, taxi driver, hair dresser, meat cutter, garbage collector, cable television operator, road worker, or even physician.

Effectiveness is a quality best tested in the marketplace. Government should stick to prosecuting fraud, misrepresentation, abuse, theft, property destruction, and other rights violations.

What about such fields as space exploration, resource management, and medical research? Don't they take a great deal of planning and money? Yes, they do. But that does not change the equation. Other individuals cannot be officially locked out of competing in those areas; they can only be kept from threatening or abusing another's property by dangerous or detrimental actions.

(It is a different question to ask whether it is the business of government to initiate any positive action in these fields. If funds for those activities were voluntarily received, then such a private setup conforms to The Allocation Principle, at least. The high visibility of government operations can assist the general advertisement of such endeavors. But if funds are not voluntarily received - as in those taken from general tax revenues - then the revenues for such enterprises have been gathered outside the ethical context of voluntary exchange and are an extension of theft and extortion. No legitimate activity can be financed with such money. Whether government has monopoly power in such fields, however, is clearly answerable in the negative.)

The history of NASA in the 1980s clearly demonstrates how a monopoly can discourage and crush all non-sanctioned efforts in a field.

The private space industry in this country suffocated under the protective legislation passed at NASA's request. After NASA's own mismanagement culminated in disaster, there were no competing enterprises capable of continuing space development. Space related services in *other* countries had to take up the slack.

Regarding resource managment, it should be noted that certain ecological regulation is entirely consistent with The Allocation Principle. The protection of clean air, water supplies, etc., is essential to everyone's well-being. It may be, however, that the libertarian concept of "Stewardship through Ownership" is the most effective way of preserving our precious resources, from pristine lakes to managed forests to whales in the open sea. If the definition of legitimate property were extended to include water, air, and even properly identified wildlife, and pollution was considered criminal trespass, the environment would be safeguarded to a much greater extent than under the current programs of "regulated pollution and deforestation" practiced by government agencies and corporate interests. The efforts of environmental activists should be in returning governmental lands (over 50% of all land area in most U. S. states) to "the common" from where homesteaders, conservation clubs, wilderness entrepreneurs, and responsible businesses can begin to utilize them in the most beneficial and ecologically sound manner possible.

Regarding medical research, the trend is already toward massive private investments in such promising fields as biogenetics. The need for government assistance seems minimal. But in such areas as vaccines which protect the general population against epidemic diseases, public support, if necessary, seems the prudent course. The area of health and safety is a special one, involving many third party consequences and issues of self-defense. It must be treated with a great deal of prudence and care. At the root is the right to pursue one's own self-responsible well-being *within* a community setting. Cooperation is in everyone's interest.

What about monetary control? Whatever is in the public interest is of interest to modern regulators. The problem is that every economic category - wealth, employment, wages, technology, diversification, etc. - is in the public's interest. If government were to involve itself in all these areas, it would become society's major employer and financier. It would ultimately determine what projects received funds, the wages of every employee, who would work where and when and if they could change jobs, and decide when and where individual businesses could close up shop, move, or merge with other businesses. (Note that these are functions of nearly every modern democracy.)

Obviously, a stable and identifiable currency falls into the category of "public interest." So does a currency which is directly connected to the operations of the free market. Currency and prices are more than mediums of exchange. They also provide economic information regarding supply and demand. They gauge the health of an economy in general or an industry in particular. These readable signals are an important aspect of any economic concept of stability.

Establishing a "gold standard" would assist these ends by providing a more inviolate standard than unredeemable paper. A gold standard would stop some of the counterfeiting practices government now enjoys (Federal Reserve expansion of the money supply, minting nonprecious metal coins, fiat money). But more is required: (1) banking and currency must be both denationalized *and* appropriately deregulated; (2) the government must not be able to spend money it does not have.

Most proposals for a return to the gold standard incorporate the present formula of a nationalized currency. The answer is to free currency within the concept of decentralization. Government might still retain the policing power of making certain all currency is redeemable and tied to a generally acknowledged commodity. But the right to hold gold and make it into gold coin or redeemable paper should *not* be exclusive to governments. If decentralization is not added to a return to a gold standard, government would still retain its additional powers of counterfeiting currently practiced: devaluation, deficit spending, government financed defaults.

Individuals should be able to transact business in any legitimate currency they desire. It is a logical extension of the rights of property and voluntary association. It is also a logical extension of classical-liberal economic theory. The currency which is most useful for individual needs will become dominant, just as is done in the international market. Individuals should have the ability to choose what currency is most useful to them. Insurance may even protect any risks involved. But the government should not be able to inflate, deflate, set terms of exchange, etc., at will. This is an equation for instability, bad communication, and rights transgressions. And, as modern economic historians have shown, it is an equation for recession, prolonged stagflation, and depression.

What about foreign aid? We subsidize communist nations with loans, the IMF, and direct aid, then spend billions to defend ourselves against them. We bail out Third World nations who in turn pay off bad loans from our own banks, indirectly subsidizing an already wealthy industry. It is obvious that much of our foreign aid program is illogical and counterproductive.

In addition, there are a great deal of data which suggest that even so-called benevolent foreign aid, directly given to other governments, fails in the long-term. It does not assist the actual creation of wealth. Rather, it acts as so many "transactions of decline" (to use Jane Jacobs' term) which depletes the donating country's ability to create wealth and the receiving country's ability to create a private market based on real supply-and-demand, natural resources, and private initiatives. (See P. T. Bauer's *Reality and Rhetoric: Studies in the Economics of Development*.) Aid creates dependency on more aid; it does not create an independent ability to create wealth. The capacity for independent and stable affluence is achieved only through the individual efforts of many private people in an unfettered, diverse, and decentralized market.

Foreign investment should be an individual affair. Government-to-government dealings merely perpetuate the state's domination of the countries involved. Only in the limited arena of rights protection should political associations become involved in international affairs. Commerce and communication should be left up to the individual, by right and for the long-term causes of peace and prosperity.

What about law itself? Surely the state has a monopoly on legislation. Otherwise, why bother with the state at all?

The important points to remember are: (1) sovereignty rests with individuals; and (2) the basis for law is individual rights, not legislation. Therefore, it should be noted that granting a monopoly to the state for legislative power is merely an act of expediency, not of rights. It is generally believed that it is easier to cope with one main political body instead of several. Also, a single federal structure, based on individual rights protection, can help to "reign in" over-zealous, apathetic, or corrupt local institutions. But the monopoly on legislation stems from political custom and expediency, not any rightful power inherent in the concept of political institutions. It is what we as a people are used to and what we believe we are able to utilize most effectively. If another system is devised that might be better for society in general, or for individuals of a minority, then there is no ethical or rights-oriented argument which can keep people from implementing such an experiment. The state's authority is based on individual allocations of specific rights. The state's authority can be rescinded whenever a citizenry deems it necessary.

Law is a codification of justice, of the natural rights which individuals require. Legislation is a process of defining the specific letter of that law, not of creating a new species of authority other than individual rights. "Law-making" is a process of rights identification, not people manipulation. This is the only kind of legislative function a legitimate political institution may perform.

Lastly, consider the state's monopoly on force used in law enforcement. It has been a great step forward for civilization to ban all forms of force from social interaction, except that which is necessary for immediate at-the-time-of-transgression self-defense. Not only is coercion outlawed, but "justified" retaliatory force as well. In this manner, the Hatfield-McCoy cycle of "an eye for an eye" is broken, gunslingers are unable to duel in the middle of Main Street, and all neighbors profit from the peace. Government, by taking upon itself exclusive rights to any force that is not self-defensive, protects society from potentially damaging reactionary transgressions.

An individual must be innocent until proven guilty. Lynch mobs do not determine, beyond a reasonable doubt, whether someone is guilty; and they rarely use the criterion of "first rights" to determine the criminality of any action. By making it illegal to "take the law into your own hands," by making the legal determination of all transgressions a prerogative of professional authorities, the rights of the individual are better protected. That is, if the state performs its task well. If it does not, it is ethically no better than the lynch mob.

This is a very important point. As long as our judicial and law enforcement systems satisfy us, we support them. If we become the target of governmental abuse and coercion because of judicial corruption, mismanagement, or apathy, then we have a right to look elsewhere for rights protection and law enforcement. Indeed, the monopoly on force proclaimed by the state is a form of allocated authority. It is, at root, not a state monopoly by right, but by appropriation. Like law, it is political custom and expediency that has persuaded us that government is the only arbitrator of just force. When the state fails in its job, then individuals will allocate this authority to other agencies. Essentially, force is meant to assist rights protection. If an agency other than government can help in that protection, individuals have the fundamental right to seek them out.

This is where individuals derive the authority to pay for private firms to protect life and property, including communities that employ private police to take over or assist the responsibilities of neighborhood law enforcement (often at lesser costs and greater efficiency than public authorities). This is where individuals derive the authority to, for example, solicit the help of private arbitrators to help negotiate contract disputes. In fact, there are many occassions when private agreements can be far more beneficial than public hearings and when private protection is more effective than public law enforcement.

Also, this is where the individual retains the right for citizen arrests, a vital aspect of crime control. Governmental agents are not and should not be the only agents who can work to support a legitimate Order of Justice. In fact, no rights-oriented argument can keep an individual from forcibly regaining any values that have been stolen or destroyed by an identifiable, proved transgressor. Indeed, "the law" is really *in* our hands; "civilizing" efforts designed to change or veil that reality can be the seed of tragic apathy and injustice.

Of course, every individual must be protected against coercive abuse, whether it be by a public or private law enforcer or the unbridled enthusiasm of an amateur vigilante. The rule of law - the absoluteness of "first rights" - should govern all aspects of rights enforcement. This does not mean that government must have a monopoly on force. But it does mean that the authority to use force must always come from legitimate rights and be invoked only when those rights are threatened or transgressed. For the state to claim for itself the ultimate position of authority in disputes makes things easier in many ways; but this does not mean it should make it difficult for individuals to set up their own appropriate means of solving differences and providing restitution for transgressions within a framework of "first rights."

It is an expedient use of government power to claim a position of **ultimate arbitrator** for determining the legitimate uses of force. (Then all competing forms of arbitration and restitution have one last court of appeals.) But this legitimacy comes exclusively from the individuals who have allocated this authority, nowhere else.

Legitimate government functions as a protector, not a creator or mandator. It cannot determine ends or means, that is the job of the individual. Individuals must be free to pursue their individual aims, even if they choose to do so within a system of private police protection, private courts, private insurance agreements, private restitution schemes, and a private community concept of cooperative ownership. The state cannot claim a monopoly on these things; it can only outlaw certain schemes that infringe "first rights," protect involved individuals from transgressions, and force restitution from those people responsible for criminal actions. Political associations can and should employ their own scheme, but they cannot declare it the only authorized one, nor the best or most effective. Authorization comes only from individuals; effectiveness is proved only through use.

In the last analysis, the only monopoly is the individual. Within his private sphere, the individual wields unfettered monopolistic power. Moreover, every individual possesses the right of cecession, a necessary extension of the right to self-defense. The state's insistence on geographically based "compulsory membership" is simply an illegitimate use of monopoly power.

We should not ignore the great accomplishments of our own legislative and judicial systems. Neither should we be taken in by their pronouncements of self-derived authority. The only ultimately legitimate monopoly is the individual's power over himself. No other monoply rightly exists.

If government would allow competition in the areas in which it now sanctions monopolies, the first great step in reducing the scope and cost of government could begin. The divestment of monopoly powers, the deregulation of nonecological/nonhealth concerns, and the privatization of governmental services and holdings are the initial goals envisioned by the constructive reformer. Government would not even have to actively promote the privatization of the services it presently keeps for itself; it would just have to passively renounce the monopoly status of those services - and healthy competition could begin. The result would be innovation, efficiency, decentralization, plurality, and real needs satisfaction. Justice would also be served, since rights would be recognized and protected in a more comprehensive manner and the dignity of self-responsible action would be maintained. Only then will people realize the power, flexibility, and ingenuity of a free society. Only then will people begin to understand that central control does not necessarily assist societal needs satisfaction, but has, instead, impeded real progress toward a more just and prosperous world.

Representation and Balance

Representation is a means for a political association to achieve accountability with respect to the public it is to serve. Government *must* represent the citizenry if it is to derive its authority from the citizenry. The citizenry, in turn, must demand representation to make sure their political agents are accountable to them in every way.

In modern times, this has usually meant that a political structure should include elected officials in most lawmaking positions, so that the citizenry can pick specific delegates to do their bidding as their political servants. The more elections (the more offices subjected to "political competition") the better. For the most part, this intensifies the connection between individual interests and public policy. Elections aid the cause of making government more accountable to the people.

Within the American experiment, however, the electoral process has resulted in a peculiar *coup d'Etat* for state power: buying private servitude with public funds. No guns, no Lenin, just plenty of money and favors to go around. To the modern political hopeful, American politics has become "the gentle art of getting votes from the poor and money from the rich by promising to protect each from the other" (Edward Bennett Williams). In practice, this form of "protection" translates into discretionary powers and unlimited interventionism by government on behalf of a special class. Thus, the representative "check" on state power has turned into a boon for governmental omnipotence. As Albert Jay Nock put it:

> Republicanism permits the individual to persuade himself that the State is his creation, that State action is his action, that when it expresses itself it expresses him, and when it is glorified he is glorified. The

republican State encourages this persuasion with all its power, aware that it is the most efficient instrument for enhancing its own prestige. (*Our Enemey, The State*, p. 45)

In the end, we are "lost by surrender rather than by suppression." We cannot even direct substantive criticism toward the obviously destructive aspects of State coercion since we have identified our very selves with the State. "Thus, the individual's sense of his own importance inclines him strongly to resent the suggestion that the State is by nature anti-social" (Nock).

More than "a citizenry" must be represented in a proper political association. Principles must also be represented. If modern government is to merely represent popular opinion, then only that opinion reigns. But a legitimate political association must first protect individual rights, even if that protection goes *against* popular opinion. The cornerstone of political action is, in fact, the principle of "first rights." This principle must be represented in an effective manner.

This was the purpose, in part, of the U.S. Constitution and its interpretive arm, the Supreme Court. The Constitution defined the centralizing powers of federal government and then attempted to limit that government by demanding that it perform only those powers specifically stated therein. No other powers could be granted or presumed. If any governmental agent stepped outside their defined authority, the Supreme Court could declare their action or legislation unconstitutional and, therefore, illegitimate. The problem with the Constitution was threefold: (1) it allotted to the federal government too much discretionary privilege, (2) it defined individual sovereignty in too parochial a fashion, leaving to the specific states too much authority over individual action, and (3) the limiting checks it deliniated never quite worked. Illegitimate actions from slavery to mercantile tariff regulation to nationalized paper money were permitted. Illegitimate actions from state-funded abortion to multiple taxation to compulsory governmental schooling (including the specific morality taught, the specific texts regulated, and the specific school to be attended) are presently condoned.

The first demand in the name of true political representation would be to call for adherence to the original constraints on political power formulated in the Constitution. Second, the limiting demands of a The

Allocation Principle should be recognized; rights must again be understood as inalienable individual possessions, not privileges granted by the state. The first and foremost principle represented should not be public opinion; rather, the "first rights" of each individual.

The mechanism of veto power should also be widened. The executive should have the power of a line item veto, each house should have a committee dedicated to policing its legislation with a similar power, and ratification of all new or expanded manifestations of governmental power should be subjected to majority vote by the electorate (including all new taxes, tax increases, bureaus, or functions which expand on existing political powers). The people should also have the right to dismantle any existing powers of government through the process of a "veto referendum." None of these forums (executive, legislative, or directly democratic) should be given the power to ratify *positive* obligations to governmental authority; their veto powers should be restricted to saying no to increases in state function and nothing else. If the Supreme Court were also bolstered with proper constitutional ammunition provided by The Allocation Principle, a great leap forward would be made regarding political structure and the protection of personal sovereignty.

In addition, each branch of government might include a Seat of Principle (a parliamentarian voice of conscience) which would continually set the proper agenda of government before its officials: the protection of "first rights." This Seat would also assist those officials in not deviating from their agenda.

My point is that not just people require a voice in their political associations: the clarity and restraint of the founding principles of legitimate political action must be heard at all times.

Balance, like representation, is more than a problem of internal political structure. It is a matter of balance between individual interests and the interests of political agents. The intricate checks and balances of our own federalized structure is of vital importance, but the balance that is most interesting within the context of this work is that which exists between the private and the public spheres.

Any government founded on the protection of "first rights" must recognize the **private sphere**. The private sphere begins with one's body and one's property. This includes one's opinions, labor, that which one's labor produces, all legitimate material wealth, any action which is nonaggressive, all of which must not be touched, hindered, or manipulated in any way by political action. Within a pragmatic political scenario, this includes any action not specifically designated as "unlawful" by legislative pronouncement.

The **public sphere** is the sphere of political action: legislative and offical law enforcement systems, national defense, and the bureaucracy needed to keep it all going. The sphere of public action is to confine itself to the specified tasks of rights protection and all bureaucratic tasks needed to support such protection. Yet, the public sphere must be as large or small as is required to effectively protect rights. In a harmonious and pluralistic society, this should be a limited sphere; in a chaotic and parasitical society, the public sphere would have to be more assertive and somewhat larger. It must always be aware of its duties. It must be able to expand when necessary, contract when not needed.

(An example of such an expanding/contracting public sphere is the government employed by many American Indian tribes prior to European influences. In times of crisis, leaders were sought by the tribe to plan strategies, lead warriors, organize expeditions, speak at counsels, etc. These leaders were chosen mainly by merit and their leadership roles lasted only as long as necessary and were always dependent upon the consent of tribal members. General law enforcement was a shared inter-tribal obligation; ostracism was the major punishment. Similar expanding/contracting public spheres could be observed among Celtic and early Germanic tribes, where self-responsible sovereignty was demanded by an individualistic people and the major economic mode was decentralized nomadic hunting - a difficult system for permanent rulers to exploit.)

Regarding the balance of spheres, the first and most necessary aspect is that the line between what is private and what is public must be easily definable. It cannot be blurred and unpredictable. This is accomplished when the tasks of political institutions are specific and limited, when laws are predictable and coherent, when they are applied equally to all and do not mandate means or ends, and when enforcement procedures are known and legitimate. If the boundaries become hard to distinguish, public and private action can become fatally intertwined.

It is in the interest of every freedom loving individual to keep the private sphere as large as possible and as clearly defined as possible. It must be distinctly separate from any political function or power. The private sphere is the single most powerful balance against political excess and coercion. In fact, the size and officially recognized legitimacy of the private sphere is what actually determines the true extent of one's liberty. The reason is that **rights and liberty *are* the private sphere.**

It is interesting to note that some people believe the private sphere to be sufficient by itself. They cogently argued for a society in which there is no public sphere whatsoever. (See, for example, Morris and Linda Tannehill's *The Market for Liberty*.) I do not wish to quarrel with these arguments, except perhaps with their utopian nature; they are invaluable in their ability to point out the spontaneous machinery of freedom that already exists in society. How I have defended the existence of a public sphere is by defining it as the protector of the individual against the collectivist and hierarchical demands of society. If a society existed that had no such demands, then the private sphere might be sufficient. If human beings could behave morally and rationally toward each other, there might be no need to instutitute the constraints of government among them. If a Politics of Rights could be maintained without a unifying national identity, a republican procedure of lawmaking, and a final court of appeals, then society might be better off government-free. In addition, if a society could exist wherein private associations and free market functions were able to protect a population against international enemies, then the private sphere would not need augmenting. Until that (rather improbable) time, the importance of the private sphere must be articulately advanced and the proper function of the public sphere must by defined and vigilantly limited; and the differences between them must never be forgotten.

Restitution, Not Punishment

The purpose of law is not to punish criminals or exact revenge upon them for any "moral sin" they may have committed. It is not to rehabilitate them to more "normal" styles of living. It is simply to gain from them restitution for their crime.

When an individual has abridged another's rights, he must restore that individual, as best as possible, to his state prior to the transgression. This is what political agents are to oversee. They should not slap the transgressor's hand or in any way demoralize him. That is not the point of justice. What is in question is the victim's confiscated or destroyed values and his capacity for self-responsible life-making. They are to be reinstated. Once this is accomplished (and restitution has been made to the law enforcement process for costs, if appropriate), then the case is closed.

If, however, the criminal is destitute, or if the transgression took on the form of some permanent destruction (like murder or maiming), then the issue becomes more complicated. But the basic principles do not change. A criminal should never be made the slave of a victim, of a victim's heirs, or of society in general. The destitute criminal should make his best effort to compensate for his transgression, which may involve some sort of work-restitution program under private or public supervision. Yet, he should also be able to support himself (even if in a moderate fashion). As for the murderer, he must compensate those who are affected by the loss of the deceased (by paying a monetary settlement or engaging in some other appropriate compensating action). This may involve a very long process, and the murderer may spend the good share of his life compensating for this severe transgression. But he must also be protected from heirs who might take advantage of his position. The principle of restitution must remain paramount in either case, balanced with the ethical absolute of inviolate human dignity.

Although violent crime amounts to only 10% of all rights transgressions, in these cases restitution may not be the only answer. The threat of continued violence may prompt a community to ostracize the transgressor. This is the justification for prisons and deportation. But prisons are all too often asylums of pure boredom in which the only lessons are those which teach aggressive and irresponsible behavior. They are nothing more than legally sanctioned arenas for social retribution against the "morally depraved." They should, instead, be places where individual liberty is as great as possible, under the specific circumstances; where inmates can engage in entrepreneurial activities with the outside world, when feasible (so that real restitution can occur); and where private property is still protected, as far as circumstances permit. It must never be construed that ostracism or imprisonment absolves the criminal from his obligation of compensation.

Victor Hugo, in his classic *Les Miserables*, showed the inhumane nature of retribution and punishment. For stealing a loaf of bread, Jean

Valjean (Hugo's main character) spends the majority of his life in prison. Hugo reacts by stating in his narration, "What a mournful moment is that in which society withdraws itself and gives up a thinking being for ever." This is what happens when law becomes an arm of punishment instead of an arm of justice.

Law is meant to protect potential victims, nothing else. Any other interpretation gives to society nasty powers of public humiliation and character manipulation. Only restitution brings home the point of self-responsibility and the dignity of each human being, victim and transgressor alike. Punishment merely fosters resentment; restitution enables the criminal to atone for his crime in a constructive and forthright manner.

This position, however, must not be construed as being "soft" on criminals. Indeed, requiring compensation is a very serious matter, involving far more time and labor than most punishment schemes currently employed.

Also, the practice of letting criminals off because uncoerced yet incriminating evidence is legally inadmissible is an outrage to the concept of justice. As William Buckley, Jr., suggested in his classic book, *Four Reforms*, "Procedures should adapt to the criterion: Did he do it?" Of course, an individual should never be *made* to testify against himself (or anyone else, for that matter), since knowledge and opinion are each man's inviolate possession. And no evidence should be admissible if obtained under torture or threats of any kind. But if true justice is our goal, criminals must be prosecuted and victimized values restored.

Liability, Not Immunity

As a direct result of isonomy, lawmakers and law enforcers must be judged by the same law and in the same manner as everyone else. This means that they must be responsible for their actions, just as everyone else must be.

All governmental employees should be liable for any wrongs they commit. Neither the police chief nor the President should be able to claim immunity, not in a legitimate government. They can never be immune to the obligation of providing compensation for their transgressions, accidental or intentional. Law is not relative to status; all men are equal before it.

Individuals should have the right to sue any political agency or agent. In fact, such suits should be encouraged. In this manner, one more level of accountability is added to the political process. Monetary rewards should be taken from general agency funds when the agency in general is liable. They should be payed for by the responsible agents when individual agents are liable. Above all, victims must be compensated for being victimized. The individuals who make up government cannot be shielded by privilege from responsibility.

Noncoercive Revenue

The Allocation Principle exposes taxation as an illegitimate power of government. Due to this fundamental illegitimacy existing at the very heart of governmental structure, Frederic Bastiat stated one hundred years ago, "The state is the great fictitious entity by which everyone seeks to live at the expense of everyone else." Alan Burris presents the problem in contemporary terms:

> Would you sign a blank contract with someone who wouldn't tell you what, if anything, you would get, or how much you will be charged -- one who just says, "trust me"? That's the "deal" you get from government. (*A Liberty Primer*)

Yet, if I am to recommend the existence of political associations while at the same time denounce taxation, I must be able to show ways political agencies might gain revenues which enable them to perform their limited, although often costly, functions.

It must first be realized that the scope of proper and legitimate political activities would be much less than what is practiced by any governmental institution now in power. Expenditures would be less, accordingly. By abolishing most regulatory bureaucracies, firing the IRS, and denationalizing the majority of the welfare apparatus; by stopping our world-policing foreign policy and our subsidization of half the world's militaries; by ceasing to subsidize foreign governments, the

U.N., large banks, corporations, the farming and steel industries, considerable savings could be found. In addition, a market free of regulation would be able to save a great deal of expense and time, become more competitive, diverse, innovative, efficient, decentralized, resulting in the wider dispersal of a greater, increasing wealth. If political agents stuck to rights protection as their single function, budgets could be procured in very noncoercive ways and the general welfare of society would be greatly enhanced.

The first concept in acquiring noncoercive revenues would be paying for services. Contracts and formal labor agreements should carry with them a percentage user fee which would pay for policing and protecting them under the laws of the land. Exceptions must be made, with proper arrangements, for those who could not afford the fee, since every individual must have the right of protection regardless of ability to pay. But the "protection fee" would assist in paying for the legal machinery reguired to protect everyone's contractual rights, augmenting an appropriate scheme of "restitution to the courts" paid by those who break the terms of their contracts (see below). Contracting parties who join in the most costly agreements pay the most, as a flat percentage, but they also have the most to loose.

Other services, such as National Guard rescue operations and the policing of communities, should charge for their services when feasible, at a rate within the means of each citizen. This would not only make the services more accountable to the public it serves, it would also enlighten the public to the services available to it.

Also, citizen legislators and their staffs should not be paid through a generalized revenue scheme, but directly by their constituents. They should be able to work at outside jobs while serving office and/or draw on any savings they have accrued prior to taking office. Since political agencies would have no powers of privilege or economic intervention, such a liberal employment system would not expose an individual lawmaker to any indiscrete temptations. It should be noted that many senators, for example, are already millionaires, so their constituents wouldn't *have* to pay them anything. (This includes the payment of pensions, business expenses, foreign junkets, etc.)

Of course, *no* services we presently receive are, by any stretch of the imagination, "free." We as taxpayers pay for everything our many levels of government do. The difference between taxation and this payment scheme (paying political agents directly for services rendered) removes the coercive element from political revenues by making them voluntary and decentralized. It puts the purse strings squarely in the hands of the people, no longer filtered through an official, centralized, and potentially elitist House of Representatives (or County Board or Town Council or Mayor's office).

Along these same lines, the second principle of noncoercive revenue would be **restitution to the court**, by the losing party, for court costs. This would also be subject to considerations of the party's ability to pay and may have to be dispersed over an appropriate period. But it is only proper that those who abuse the rights of individuals should themselves pay for the administration of law brought on, for the most part, by their own predatory actions. Criminals should pay for what their actions have cost the system (which, in many cases, would exceed the amount of restitution due the victim). Regarding contract disputes, if a private arbitration and fee structure were determined ahead of time as the negotiating mechanism, then payment to government courts would be applicable only if that system were used in appeals.

The third principle of noncoercive revenue is **voluntary donations**. This includes such devices as telethons, ad campaigns, and fund drives. Pleas for these donations would have to appeal to our interests and compassion and be based on rational persuasion. Money would be directly tied to perceived need and individual interest. Fund drives for the military, for the restoration of monuments and public buildings, and for charity programs (if such programs still existed in the public sphere) would be common place. Witnessing the success of emergency drives for numerous relief programs demonstrates the effec - tiveness of these campaigns. Not only is it a way of gaining noncoercive revenue, it is also a way of informing the public about political programs and binding citizens together in common cause. It is one more way for individuals to make political associations accountable to the citizenry.

Voluntary labor would also go under this heading, since many individuals have more time on their hands than money and would be willing to perform educational, counseling, bookkeeping, and other duties necessary to a community organization. Witness the efforts in voluntary relief programs, the involvement in emergency aid initiatives, the energy currently shown by political volunteers during campaigns, etc. When a cause is deemed honorable or beneficial, volunteers abound.

The fourth principle is simply **earning money.** Political associations should invest any excess they receive in a safe yet productive manner. They should be free to run lotteries, bake-offs, fairs, contests, firemen's balls, and the like. This is a great way to involve a community in, say, raising money for a local police budget. But efforts to invest or raise large sums must attempt to minimize their impact on the normal workings of the free market. Next to the problem of withdrawing money from private enterprise, the worst ill taxation brings to a society is the way it distorts an economy with subsidies and tax shelters. This must not happen when legitimate political agents seek to raise their own revenue.

There are many more ideas that would satisfy the need for noncoercive revenue. These are only a few. My point is that money can be raised without legalizing theft. Making political associations raise their revenue noncoercively is the most potent means of keeping them in touch with and accountable to the citizens they are meant to serve. Political action truly becomes a tool of the people when funded by consent. Society is brought together in common cause - not torn apart by programs which fail to serve it fairly and are funded by compulsory taxation.

Indeed, this is the greatest fear modern politicians have: making their revenue tied to public approval. Compulsory tax withholding is only 40 years old, yet the idea of returning to a voluntarily reported and voluntarily paid tax system is laughed at as impossible. Why? Taxpayers simply would not stand for the high cost governmental prerogative now costs them - if they had a direct choice in the matter. Other more inventive schemes, such as letting a taxpayer designate which portion of his taxes should be paid into which agency, a scheme which would make an individual's taxes tied more closely to his interests and goals, are dismissed out of hand as not only unworkable but somehow anti-social. Even the moral demand to require a balanced budget, so that we stop forcing onto future generations the exorbitant bill for our present indulgences, has all but died.

Compulsory taxation forces every citizen to pay for all functions of government, whether they agree with those functions or not. But forcing individuals to pay for things which they consider indecent is itself indecent. Said Thoreau, regarding his own tax evasion, "I do not care to trace the course of my dollar, if I could, till it buys a man, or a musket to shoot one with - the dollar is innocent - but I am concerned to trace the effects of my allegiance." We want to give our allegiance only to activities we consider right and just. This could be done by tracing the "innocent dollar" directly from the individual to the political agency or service in question. Until that time, "allegiance" will be a matter of compulsion and not a true extension of a free and satisfied people.

The single reason simple and self-sufficient life styles are fading from the U. S. landscape (such as family farms, the independent and self-reliant businessman, inner city neighborhood cooperatives, communal American Indian communties) is that they have collapsed under the weight of skyrocketing property taxes, the inflating burden of social security taxes, the increasingly complex mixture of city, county, state, and federal taxes (which take 57% of the average taxpayer's income), and the many requirements IRS and other regulations force upon businesses and individuals alike (bookkeeping, filing, disclosure procedures, lawyer fees, etc.) Politics in the New Age must protect these people from the dream-crushing weight of the many-headed Hydra called compulsory taxation. There must be a place in this great country for every dream to blossom, not just those proposed by corporate statists. Government must be stopped from devouring Self-responsible Man. The most immediate deterrent, and one which has the broadest appeal, is to simply tighten its purse strings.

In Conclusion

The proper functions of political associations are seen to be (1) law identification and enforcement and (2) national security - both summarized in the concept of rights protection. In every political function, government must be accountable to individual rights, to the "first rights" of every citizen.

It should be noted that one can advocate a system of political action similar to the Politics of Rights without necessarily agreeing with me on every point. Political sovereignty is a concept which can be arrived at from various directions.

For example, religious doctrines may demand a recognition of individual rights and a limited government. Some religions may demand no governmental interference in the social order whatsoever. Instead of relying on prudent humanistic arguments, a responsible interpretation of theological doctrine may yield the same results. (Patrick Henry, one of the greatest libertarian orators, was an ardent Christian, unlike his deist contemporaries - Washington, Jefferson, Madison, Paine, and others. But it was Henry's unpretentious and hardworking evangelicalism which drove him to speak out against the aristocratic extravagance of centralized government and to advocate the straightforward virtues of independence and voluntarism.)

Also, pragmatic economic models demonstrate that a minimal government protecting property rights within a free market is the best way to create wealth and to alleviate poverty and inequality. Economists arrive at these conclusions not from a rights perspective, but from a utilitarian perspective. (The intellectual voyage of someone like F. A. Hayek is of note: he began as a socialist, concerned with the the well-being of individuals within society, believing the best path toward a better future lay with a more comprehensive application of democratic socialism. When pragmatic arguments, along with his own economic research and honest insight, indicated that he was wrong, he enthusiastically embraced the libertarian-conservative point of view.)

This broad appeal in no way diminishes the attractiveness of the Politics of Rights. In fact, this underscores its ability to satisfy the needs of all people who value the concepts of self-responsibility, value-achievement, personal liberty, social justice, and economic opportunity.

PRACTICALITY AND PROGRESS

Practicality is usually determined *with respect to specific circumstances*: that which is possible within one's perceived situation. It is associated with no principle except utility. Other principles, such as ethical ones, are employed to determine the *goals* practical steps are meant to achieve. Practicality merely determines the safest, most efficient and circumstantially feasible ways to achieve those goals.

If our socio-political goals are individual needs satisfaction and rights protection, then a second question must be asked: What is the most *practical* way to achieve these goals? If free commerce within a protected Order of Consonance can achieve the most efficient needs satisfaction and rights protection for society, then that is what is the most *practical* system for a society to employ - if it is possible with respect to present circumstances.

The next question becomes: Is socio-political liberty circumstantially possible? Two obstacles present themselves: the nature and will of man. If man, because of his short-sighted, egocentric, aggressive, ignorant nature simply cannot live in harmony with his fellow man within a context of freedom, then political liberty is indeed impractical. If his nature, in general, is up to the task but his desire, in specific, falls short, then liberty could not be sustained even if it was achieved. Political liberty becomes a vain exercise in the short run, impractical in the long.

My answer to the first obstacle is that man *can* live in harmony with his fellow man, requiring only minimal constraints, *in spite* of himself. Political constraints are central - as deterrents, as stabilizing mechanisms, as disciplining habits - and cannot be dismissed. But harmony and needs satisfaction often come from unintentional sources. Because man cares more for himself than his neighbor, he is more apt to be productive, more apt to be protective of his rights, and more apt to be tolerant of his fellow man: the self-interest inherent in capitalism produces goods in excess of any other economic system; the free market's dependence on property and contract law forces its participants to honor individual rights; and policing a neighbor's beliefs is not only superfluous but wasteful with regard to one's self-centered pursuit of personal satisfaction. The lackluster ideal of "tit for tat" does more to promote social peace and honest reciprocity than any moralizing could.

In fact, most "moral" endeavors end in restrictive intolerance and coercive utopias.

The Politics of Rights takes better advantage of man's egocentric "short-comings" than any other political system. In light of man's nature, it becomes the most practical political option.

But do human beings have sufficient *will* for liberty? Can they break the chains of coercive habit? Can they look beyond today and see the promise, the potential? Do they have the rational skills and emotional desire to monitor their progress and adjust to new circumstances? Do they have the confidence to rely on the power within themselves, to stop being victims, to come into there own, to take up their own lives without taking over someone else's?

My answer, all things considered, is a rather disheartened "No, we do not have sufficient will." Not yet, anyway.

Perhaps in our fear of the unknown, our fear of our own individual and collective ignorance, and our fear of attempting anything new, we distort practicality to mean: that which is possible without changing any aspect of the existing order. But the existing order includes a high degree of violence and manipulation, overt and covert coercion, social injustice and legislated inequality. Does being practical mean we have to live with the negative aspects of the status quo?

Practicality should determine the methods we utilized to achieve our desires. The limits of practicality should be determined by the *potentials* that exist within physical reality, human nature, and an ethical code of conduct, not merely by what *is*. The most practical political solutions to our present problems are not found in continued authoritarian centralization, nor will they be met effectively through greater liberal regulation; rather, they will be found within the context of free commerce, rights protection, and the rule of universal sovereignty. An expanded free market, supported by the Politics of Rights, becomes the most practical way to achieve social harmony, needs satisfaction, and the protection of the private sphere of individual action.

Progress, like practicality, is a term greatly distorted and maligned by the opponents of freedom. Progress is merely a concept relative to what one wants to achieve. If you are moving toward your goal, you are progressing. Progress is not merely change. Change for the sake of change may be an aspect of human invention and intellectual pursuit, but change for the sake of progress is change which has the potential of moving one closer to that which one desires.

Progress requires a vision of what life should be, or at least of what a better life should entail. For one's own distinct life, this vision grows out of one's sense of life and self, becoming the concept of selfestness - a driving moral ambitiousness and desire for self-fulfillment. For a society, this vision consists only of guiding principles and generalities which support harmony and prosperity. Both these individual and social visions are continually changing, adjusting to the unforeseen intellectual and material changes within society. But for the one to nurture the other, the dynamics of individual liberty and the security of the rule of law is required.

When government takes it upon itself to legislate the means and ends of individual lives, it appropriates to itself the power to define practicality and progress. It determines what actions can and cannot be done, not merely what are rights transgressions. It determines what is safe, what actions will get you what you want, and what circumstances you will be acting within. It determines the circumstances and content of commerce, education, and innovation. In the process, it determines what society should become, even in the particular, by legislating inherently static boundaries society must exists within socially, intellectually, morally, technologically, etc. The issue of practicality becomes constrained and confined by the opinions of a few politicians. Much less is practical, and when that is the case, much less becomes possible. The issue of progress necessarily conforms to the opinions of a few politicians who are, ultimately, unable to foresee the exact consequences of their actions. Rational practicality is replaced by state mandates, and real progress, for real people, is mortally inhibited.

This is a serious criticism of more than communist oligarchies and fascist dictatorships, more than past feudal lordships or present socialistic single party systems, more than old fashion monarchies and their aristocratic courts. It is an indictment of all modern social democracies - even modern democratic republics like our own.

Ignorance and Liberty

> All political theories assume that most individuals are very ignorant. Those who plead for liberty differ from the rest in that they include among the ignorant themselves as well as the wise. (F. A. Hayek, *The Constitution of Liberty*)

Liberty is the state in which individuals are able to choose for themselves. Coercion is the state in which those in authority determine what their subjects will choose.

I have argued that social consonance founded on individual liberty is the only legitimate goal for an ethical political theory (embodied in the notion of "rights protection") because of the **positive requirements of man's nature**: his innate need for self-responsible action and his noble desire to protect and extend the integrity of his self-creative values. Hayek comes to the same conclusion about liberty but from a different viewpoint. He asserts that liberty is a *practical* political goal because of the **limitations of man's nature** within the complexity of modern society:

> **Civilization begins when the individual** in pursuit of his ends can make use of more knowledge than he himself acquired and when he **can transcend the boundaries of his own ignorance by profiting from knowledge he does not possess** [or even knows exists].
>
> The knowledge which any individual mind consciously manipulates is only a small part of the knowledge which at any one time contributes to the success of his action. **When we reflect how much knowledge possessed by other people is an essential condition for the successful pursuit of our individual aims, the magnitude of our ignorance of the circumstances on which the results of our action depend appears simply staggering.** Knowledge exists only as the knowledge of individuals. It is not much

better than a metaphor to speak of the knowledge of society as a whole. The sum knowledge of all individuals exists nowhere as an integrated whole. **The great problem is how we can all profit from this knowledge, which exists only disposed as the separate, partial, and sometimes conflicting beliefs of all men.**

In other words, it is largely because civilization enables us constantly to profit from knowledge which we individually do not possess and because each individual's use of his particular knowledge may serve to assist others unknown to him in achieving their ends that men as members of a civilized society can pursue their individual ends so much more effectively than they could alone.

Our attitude, when we discover how little we know of what makes us cooperate, is, on the whole, one of resentment rather than of wonder and curiosity. Much of our occasional impetuous desire to smash the whole entangled machinery of civilization is due to this inability of man to understand what he is doing.
(*The Constitution of Liberty*)

The rule of philosopher kings, of bureaucratic specialists, or any other form of "centralized wisdom" does not work because no one person or small group of people can possibly *know enough* to make decisions for an entire society - its ecomony, its legal demands, its unforeseen technological innovations. It is not just that such a system would be immoral - it would be ineffective and unable to achieve its aims of peace and prosperity.

> It is only when such exclusive rights are conferred on the presumption of superior knowledge of particular individuals or groups that the process [of progress] ceases to be experimental and beliefs that happen to be prevalent at a given time may become an obstacle to the advancement of knowledge.

> The argument for liberty is not an argument against organization, which is one of the most powerful means that human reason can employ, but an argument against all exclusive, privileged, monopolistic organization, [an argument] against coercion to prevent others from trying to do better. (Hayek)

Vast evidence exists which demonstrates that a decentralized free market achieves the greatest degree of economic opportunity and prosperity as well as personal freedom and choice. Why don't politicians and the electorate recognize these facts? It is a belief that a few can decide for the rest of us not merely what is most profitable, but what is most *right*.

If the wise and well-intentioned among us take up the power of deciding our futures for us, it will be no less disastrous than if we were to be oppressed by a blind and sinister tyrant. Both paths lead to a legislation of means and ends, to a willful molding of one life by another, to coercion. Both paths constrict progress by outlawing individual invention and private pursuits. Both paths limit the creation and dissemination of new knowledge, discourage experimentation, and retard both social and economic prosperity. Both paths replace self-responsibility with subservience to authority. Both paths destroy the spontaneous structure of an interdependent society.

It is prudent to stop neighbors from tinkering with nuclear warheads in their basement and jeopardizing numerous third party rights - this is a proper use of regulatory law. But those who would reshape society into their own utopian image are more than fools doomed to failure, they are the Great Exploiters who plunder our futures for a chance to exercise their "wisdom" and who trade our own individual power (to which they have no right) for their own political rewards. Under the rule of exploiters, individuals will not only lose economic freedom, but the ability for general self-fulfillment. The Great Exploiters' greatest theft is authentic, self-nourishing progress.

> Progress does not mean greater happiness; rather, greater ability to deal with our present obstacles, a process of learning, an enjoyment of the capacity for intelligence and "movement for movement's sake"

which enables success to gain a higher probability of occurring. (Hayek)

The limits of human reason and the existence of immense human ignorance does not mean that centralized coercion in the form of a wise and benevolent state is needed to make peace, justice, and prosperity a reality. In fact, **the limits of human reason and the ignorance of individuals requires a general state of liberty to exist**, so that knowledge can be shared along lines of mutual benefit, economic progress can proceed fast enough to be experienced by a maximum number of people, and the sphere of what is practical and possible is broadened within the context of voluntary association and individual rights. Without liberty, progress cannot exist. And without progress, the virtue of moral ambition will seem an impossible and impractical human characteristic, and the engine of man will run down to a very slow idle, or, perhaps, be stopped altogether.

Exploitation and Regulation

Exploitation is the act of turning something not in one's legitimate possession to one's own use by taking advantage of the legitimate owner's lack of rank, knowledge, or prowess. People can be taken advantage of by exploiting their physical or mental weaknesses, their ignorance, unskillfulness, age, naivete, economic situation, low self-esteem, or some other circumstantial or permanent handicap. People and possessions can be illegitimately turned to one's own use by coercive actions such as expropriation, extortion, misrepresentation (including fraud, lying, breaking promises), subtle and overt intimidation, outright theft, economic or psychological slavery, breaking contracts, etc. This also includes manipulative regulations not associated with rights protection (such as those codified by the CAB, ICC, FTC, FCC, BIA, IRS, and most of those demanded by the SEC, FEC, DEA, and DOE, to name but a few) - regulations which are outside the sphere of health, safety, and ecological concerns protecting appropriate *third party* rights and *nonconsenting* involvements.

Much of the Marxist doctrine was designed to criminalize exploitation and regulate the circumstances which lead to exploitation. This is its greatest appeal. But Marx did not define exploitation properly. He viewed "profiting from another's labor" as exploitive and sought to outlaw exploitation by expropriating the economic system of profit-making. If all production were owned by the state, he reasoned, then individual capitalists would be unable to exploit the labor of unpropertied workers. If all aspects of social interaction were channelled through the state, society's interests would then be the state's interests and "free" individuals would act, for the first time, for the benefit of all.

The problem with this reasoning is twofold: first, it implies that the state is a nonexploitive apparatus; and, second, that profit-making is inherently exploitive. Both assumptions are wrong. The state, in fact, is the most centralized agent of exploitation in existence, while the free market is the most potent advocate of noncoercion. By crippling the latter and giving absolute power to the former, a Marxist society ends up being the most exploitive in the history of civilization, making all individuals the victim of political exploitation.

Within a free market, an individual owns his life and labor. He may contract out his labor for money, returned services, or for any other noncoercive agreement he might set. The producer who contracts with the laborer benefits from that labor, but not necessarily in any exploitive fashion. By selling a product for a profit (a product being a mixture of the laborer's labor with materials and production design owned by the producer), the producer is able to pay the laborer, invest in his own productive system, and pay himself. If the laborer felt he was not getting a self-beneficial deal, he could move on to a new job or negotiate for a new contract. He will always own his own labor. But he does not have a *right* to profits, unless he is part owner or an arrangement of profit-sharing was agreed to in advance. He is due only what is stipulated in his legitimate contract. If the contract is kept, he gains a known and desired benefit. No exploitation necessarily enters into the relationship.

Consider the countries where the state owns and regulates production. Do the laborers own their own labor? May they freely negotiate their contracts? May they work for whom they wish? May they quit their present job and move on when desired? May they accumulate capital, borrow capital, or become independent producers without the state's consent? What happens when the state does not consent?

The state can easily be seen as the major exploiter of laborers and producers alike within these oppressively centralized regimes.

What about the less oppressive social democracies in which relatively few industries are directly *owned* yet most all industries are heavily *regulated* by the state? Does this make for a less exploitive situation?

State regulation, although less Marxist at first glance than state ownership, is none the less *a form of state ownership.* Ownership involves the right of use and disposal. **Those who determine use and disposal of property are the real owners in a society, regardless of what lip-service regulators pay to "legal title" so to appease the populace. Those who regulate the ends and means of other people's lives are the real exploiters, regardless of what lip-services is paid to isolated "personal freedoms" a citizenry may be granted.**

Marx himself understood that the exploitation of a people cannot effectively begin until their lands and properties have been expropriated. The "genius" of modern democracies is in how they have replaced the more archaic forms of forced confiscation with expropriating regulations. The social result, however, is no less exploitive.

The justification for regulation is ignorance. It is believed that people either do not know, are unable to decide, or cannot accomplish that which is in their best long-term interest. To the regulator, ignorance requires regulation - to "help people along." Of course, this means that the regulator does not include himself among the ignorant, since he must have the answers. He is worthy to regulate because he is wiser than the rest.

> The theory of regulation incorrectly assumes: 1) that we wouldn't voluntarily do what is best for us even if we knew; 2) that there are superior beings who know far better that we do what is best for us; 3) that these omniscient persons can and will be selected for positions of authority by us inferiors; 4) that these saintly people will defy human nature and decide what is best for us rather than what is best for themselves; 5) that they will make fewer mistakes than we would; 6) that laws and regulations actually work as intended without serious harmful side effects. If any *one* of

these assumptions is untrue, then logically we should not entrust the direction of our lives to government. And they are *all* false! (Alan Burris, *A Liberty Primer*)

Actually, regulation is more than the wise deciding what is best for us. It is often explained as a way of stopping people from committing crimes before they have the chance. But things that are criminal (violations of our property rights) are already crimes. We should be protected against them by law, not coerced into acting certain ways that are deemed appropriate by state authority. When crimes are perpetrated, the criminals involved should be brought to justice and the victims should be compensated.

Why regulate *law abiding citizens* with red tape and bureaucratic meddling when these people would not perpetrate any crimes in the first place? This is an abridgement of the rights to freedom from coercion and the right to private, noncoercive action. As for the criminal, they will break the law, regardless of regulation. Regulations only make their job easier, since they add governmental bribes to their bag of tricks and because the rest of us become more placid and naive, distanced from self-responsibility, and constrained from direct action under regulation.

> **Regulation and prosecution of crime are quite different things...** Regulation is an attempt to control innocent, peaceful people's behavior according to the views of those in power. It creates the artificial crime of failing to obey the orders of politicians, that is, a *political crime...* There are *no* victims when regulation is broken, except possibly bureaucrats with hurt feelings... Regulation hurts only honest people.
>
> Crimes are violations of our property rights... There is a victim who deserves restitution. [But] the theory of regulation [is] correctly understood simply as attempts to justify exploitation...

> To benefit from exploitation, it is necessary to avoid becoming the victim of exploitation by others. But once the practice is established, there is no principle to exclude others who will want "theirs." So we have a system in which, to some degree, everyone exploits everyone else.
>
> No one has the right to regulate another person on the theory that he/she *might* commit a crime. Only when an attack is imminent or underway does the victim or the victim's agent have the right to use force in self-defense. (Burris)

Regulation *is* coercive force. Regulation forces everyone to perform certain actions, legislating and codifying means and ends, bending individuals to the will of the regulator. The reasons are never self-defensive, unless being protected from competition and innovation is viewed as self-defense.

Note that most all regulation is requested and/or controlled within the regulated industry. Citrus growers are regulated by laws lobbied for by the largest producers in the industry. Unions are protected and regulated by laws proposed by the largest and oldest unions in the country. Import quotas are suggested by the industries they are designed to protect. The AMA has power to regulate its own, as do hair-stylists, truckers, meat-cutters. The list is almost endless. Why is this so? Because regulation is an excellent mechanism of privilege: it supplies an advantage to well established groups, protects others outright, and endows regulators with incredible discretionary powers. Regulation is simply the power of exploitation - whereas **the free market** (a regulator's greatest nemesis) **is**, essentially, **the will of the people.** (Burris)

Also note that the sectors of economic activity which are presently outlawed or completely regulated - such as illegal drug production and distribution, prostitution, gambling, trading in nonofficial currencies, etc - are the areas of highest criminality. The fiasco of alcohol prohibition is an excellent example of this phenomenon. Due to regulatory law, the outlawed industries are no longer subjected to the competitiveness of the free market, are cut off from the administration of property rights and contract law (few prostitutes, for example, would seek damages from their pimps because it would be self-incriminating), and, since we think the government is handling the problem for us in these areas, they are cut off, for the most part, from personal involvement by interested law abiding individuals. Regulation has insulated these economic areas - "protected" them from all but inefficient, centralized, understaffed, and potentially corrupt state policing. Exploitation by the criminal element is able to run rampant.

Regulation creates two Great Exploiters: (1) those who use the political apparatus to exploit others for their own gain (politicians, bureaucrats, and industrial regulators), and (2) those who exploit others within the areas protected from free market activity (organized crime and small time pimps, drug dealers, loan sharks, etc.)

If you think you are free of exploitation *because of* governmental regulation, try building a safe and cost efficient home or garage on your land that does not adhere to governmental codes, try fighting the government when it evokes its eminent domain powers and rams a four lane highway through your farm, try talking your way out of an anti-trust suit, try bartering with someone without informing the IRS, try patenting an invention the government considers superfluous or nutty, try teaching your child at home without the permission of your school board, try using the services of a midwife for a home birth without the knowledge of the AMA, try broadcasting on unused airwaves, try advertising stock in your company without employing a battalion of lawyers to appease the army of corporate regulators, and if you know enough about law but have no degree, try performing the services of a lawyer. If you are destitute and need a job, try selling your labor below the "minimun wage" or working at a difficult or hazardous job that the government is trying to protect you from. If you are sick, try using a drug or procedure the FDA has not approved, even if it is your last hope. If you are bothered by air or water pollutants, try suing your local utilities to ensure your right to unpolluted property.

This sort of regulation does not protect "first rights." It does not insure freedom. It merely abridges personal liberty and creates a political apparatus capable of immense exploitation. It insulates criminals from competition and justice in outlawed endeavors that would otherwise be consentual and free economic activities. Regulation, in the modern world, has become the champion of the Great Exploiters.

The great atrocities of history were committed by non-profit organizations such as political organizations and armies. One earns a profit by helping others, not by killing them...

Self-interest is not limited to concern for more money and physical possessions. It includes anything we believe will make us happier... People who understand their self-interest are difficult to exploit, even by strong force. Therefore, exploitation...normally depends on deceiving us about what our interests are, and/or persuading us that it is wrong to act in our self-interest... This explains why exploiters try to narrow the definition of self-interest to include only money and other forms of wealth, honestly gained by production and trade. Acceptance of this narrow definition would allow exploiters who are not engaged in productive activities to maintain that they are altruists, not influenced by vulgar materialism...

Exploitation is a term...used by the enemies of liberty to suggest that there is something wrong with free voluntary trading for *mutual* advantage. But the correct meaning of exploitation is *unethically* taking advantage of another person. So it is really the enemies of liberty, the power lovers who prefer force and fraud, who are the exploiters. (Burris)

Regulation is, in the last analysis, exploitation in its most devious form.

Taming the Beast with Required Compensation

We are left with this difficult problem: it is political action which is to ultimately protect our liberty yet it is government which has the greatest potential for abridging that same liberty; it is political action which is to protect us from the predatory and collectivist demands of society yet it is government that is potentially the most thorough and potent tool for both executing and promoting those same demands. Political associations are to be the apparatus through which our "first rights" are recognized and upheld, but it is government that gathers unto itself all power to grant rights and all power to define sovereignty. Political associations are to insulate the individual from coercion so that he may pursue his own selfest life, but instead government declares itself the ultimate ethical authority and decides how life should be defined and how living must be achieved.

The problem is twofold. First, it is one of ethical philosophy: the people must recognize both their right to and capacity for personal sovereignty. Second, it is one of political science: modern political structure must be reoriented so to minimize its capacity for coercion.

Regarding both problems, the citizens of the United States of America have a head start. The tradition of constructive individualism is deep and needs only to flourish. Also, the Fifth Amendment to the Constitution contains a remarkable though forgotten clause which, if followed, would be a giant step forward for individual rights:

> Nor shall private property be taken for public use without just compensation.

If an individual takes from another, it is an illegal transgression and must be compensated for, either by returning the stolen item or by some other payback scheme. If government takes from an individual, under the present law it is considered a legal transgression, but this transgression must still be compensated for.

Nearly all governmental regulations are forms of property expropriations which, under the eminent domain clause, require compensation. Not just direct property confiscation, but all losses to property values caused by governemntal action should be compensated for. If government would be required to pay compensation for *all* its actions, it would limit those actions to the most necessary. Frivolous action would simply be too expensive.

> To see how stringent a restriction this is on government action, consider zoning. I own a parcel of land on which I intend to put up apartment buildings. The local government zones the land for single-family dwellings, greatly reducing the value of

> my land. For a private individual, this action would be illegal, since it would be taking by force a part of the bundle of property rights that make up my ownership of the land. Hence government zoning is a form of taking. Hence it can be done only if the government that enacts the zoning restrictions is prepared to compensate me for the reduction in value of my land - which is, to say the least, improbable. Under [this] reading of the eminent domain clause, virtually all existing zoning legislation is unconstitutional...

Now, consider the problem of tax collection:

> There seems little point in the IRS collecting a thousand dollars from me, then returning the money as compensation for taking it. [The] answer to this is that taxation is indeed forced taking, hence the taxpayer must be compensated, but that compensation need not be in cash. If the taxes collected are used to provide benefits to the taxpayer worth at least as much as what was collected, the taxpayer has been fairly compensated for what was taken.
>
> This imposes severe restraints on what kinds of taxes can be imposed for what purposes. Any redistributive tax, designed to change people's relative incomes, is unconstitutional, since benefits do not go to the people who are paying the tax. That includes the graduated income tax we now have. (David D. Friedman, "Taking Issue with the State," a critique of Richard Epstein's *Takings: Private Property and the Power of Eminent Domain*, in *Reason*, October 1986)

Although this reform is less than what is required with a comprehensive Politics of Rights, it is dramatic, substantive, and requires absolutely no legislation, plebiscites, or constitutional amendments. It simply requires an honest interpretation of our country's most important document.

The Free Life - The Good Life

We must not look at our institutions as unchangeable givens, as sanctified monuments which cannot be altered. To criticize is not blasphemy. To reform is not sacrilege. Political associations need not be given any more allegiance than what is given one's insurance company or bank or police department. They are political structures made by men that are meant to serve men. What should be given allegiance are the principles of selfestness, self-ownership, and freedom from coercion. Government is to protect these principles - it does not create them or grant them. Patriotism should be directed toward the nation-as-community, toward nourishing ideals; institutions are merely there to satisfy needs.

We want free, nonmonopolistic political associations which protect our own sacred lives from the individual *and* institutional exploiters of this earth; not an apparatus that is *based* on exploitation. We want a socio-political structure free of demagogues and tyrants; not an apparatus which *employs* demagogues and calls them leaders. We want a spontaneous society in which individuals forge their own futures; not a society so debilitated by government that spontaneity is replaced by centralized planning, compassion by welfarism, and self-responsibility by regulation. We want a world in which we can find pride; not one in which everyone is reduced to rule-followers and beggars.

Let us demand our lives, our minds. Let us demand to be recognized as individuals. Let us demand our rights, our liberty. Let us find a way to protect our freedom of thought and action so that we might achieve self-fulfillment.

> If you lose all respect for the rights of others, and with it your own self-respect; if you lose your own sense of right and fairness; if you lose your belief in liberty, and with it the sense of your own worth and true rank; if you lose your will and self-guidance and control over your own lives and actions, what can all

the gifts of politicians give you in return? (Auberon Herbert)

Indeed, there is a greater villain than government, a private enemy which must be combated before true and lasting progress can be made on any level. It is the abdication of selfestness. If one renounces or maligns one's selfestness, one becomes an immediate victim. This is what the predatory altruists and exploitive egotists of the world prey upon - unvigilant naivete, subservient selflessness, tempted greed. It makes tyrants and slaves of us all.

> If it is a despot you wish to dethrone, see first that his throne within you is destroyed. (Kahlil Gibran, *The Prophet*)

Life is an integrated whole. One aspect cannot be separated from the rest. Joy and self-satisfaction and liberty and intelligent action and productive responsibility and attentive compassion are all inter-linking aspects of a single human process. Ethics and politics, individual pursuits and social endeavors, self-fulfillment and voluntary association are all sides of the same coin: successful human living.

Human beings are not born free. An infant is hardly self-willed. The liberating combination of sovereignty and responsibility is learned - as cultural habits and conscious tools. It is the job of the family, the community, of all human institutions, to assist in this educational process; but more than anything, it is the product of individual experience and initiative. Internal freedom is not a freedom *from*, a lack of compulsion, or a state of unlimited license. Freedom is a power to do, to understand, to work, to will toward a chosen goal. Although they know how to rebel, children are not truly free. But their rebellion defends a very real dignity, a very real desire to be self-responsible. It is men and women who are free - freed through self-responsible sovereignty.

Sovereignty is the joyous challenge of human maturity, it is also the greatest victim of paternalistic social democracies.

Look into the faces of those under tyranny's weight - is that the look of the joyful? Liberty to them is a myth, or, worse, a realm of frightening chaos. They have been deluded by oppression and have called it security. We who are not deluded must keep the light in our own eyes, the ambition in our own minds. That is the starting point. That is the only quality which will keep us going.

Do you want human dignity above all things? Then take up your life. You are the only one who can. You are the only one who knows what to do with it once you do.

You have value in yourself. No one need grant it; it is yours already. Make it grow and prosper.

A SELECTED BIBLIOGRAPHY

Lord Acton (1834-1902), *The History of Freedom in Antiquity* (Salem NH: Ayer Co. Publishers)

Hazel E. Barnes, *An Existential Ethics* (New York: Alfred A. Knopf, 1967)

Frederic Bastiat (1801-1850), *Selected Essays on Political Economy* and *L'Etat* (Irving-on-Hudson NY: Foundation for Economic Education, Inc.)

Peter T. Bauer, *Reality and Rhetoric: Studies in the Economics of Development* (Westport CT: Greenwood Press, 1986)

Peter L. Berger, *The Capitalist Revolution* (New York: Basic Books, 1986)

Nathanial Branden, *The Psychology of Self-Esteem* (Los Angeles: Nash Publishing Corporation, 1969) and *Honoring the Self* (New York: J. P. Tarcher, 1983)

E. K. Bramsted and K. J. Melhuish, ed., *Western Liberalism*: A history in documents from Locke to Croce (London: Longman Group Limited, 1978)

Peter R. Breggin, *The Psychology of Freedom* (Buffalo NY: Prometheus Books, 1980)

Jacob Bronowski, *The Origins of Knowledge and Imagination* (New Haven: Yale University Press, 1967)

William F. Buckley, Jr., *Four Reforms* (New York: Putnam, 1973) and *American Conservative Thought in the Twentieth Century*, edited by Buckley (Indianapolis: Bobbs-Merril Educational Publishing, 1978) for "The American Heritage Series"

Alan Burris, *A Liberty Primer*, Second Edition (1983)

Albert Camus, *The Rebel* (New York: Alfred A. Knopf, 1956)

Ed Clark, *A New Beginning*, 1980 Libertarian Presidential Compaign Issues book (Cardine House, 1980)

R. L. Cunningham, ed., *Liberty and the Rule of Law* (College Station TX: Texas A&M University Press, 1979)

Douglas Den Uyl, "Freedom and Virtue," in *The Libertarian Reader*, Tibor Machan, ed., (Rowman & Littlefield, 1982); and *The Philosophic Thought of Ayn Rand* with Rasmussen

John Patrick Diggins, *The Lost Soul of American Politics* (New York: Basic Books, Inc., 1984)

René Jules Dubos, *A God Within* (New York: Charles Scribners' Sons, 1972)

Antony Flew, *Thinking About Social Thinking* (New York: Basil Blackwell); *God: A Critical Inquiry* (La Salle: Open Court); and *The Politics of Procrustes* (Buffalo: Prometheus Books)

Milton Friedman, *Capitalism and Freedom* (Chicago: University of Chicago Press, 1962) and *Free to Choose* (New York: Harcourt Brace Jovanovich, 1979)

Friederic A. Hayek, *The Constitution of Liberty* (Chicago: University of Chicago Press); and *The Road to Serfdom* (Boston: Routledge & Kegan Paul Limited)

Henry Hazlit, *Economics in One Lesson* (Norwalk CT: Arlington House, 1962)

Karl Hess, *Dear America* (New York: William Morrow & Co., 1975)

John Hospers, "Libertarianism and Legal Paternalism," in *The Libertarian Reader*, Tibor Machan, ed., (Rowman & Littlefield, 1982)

Morton A. Kaplan, *On Freedom and Human Dignity* (Morristown NJ: General Learning Press, 1973).

Israel Kirzner, *Discovery and the Capitalist Process* (Chicago: University of Chicago Press, 1986)

Paul Kurtz, *In Defense of Secular Humanism* (Buffalo: Prometheus Books, 1983)

Henri Lepage, *Tomorrow, Capitalism* (La Salle and London: Open Court, 1982)

Jim Lewis, *Liberty Reclaimed* (National Libertarian Party, 301 W. 21st, Houston TX 77008, 1984)

John Locke (1632-1704), *Two Treatises of Government* (New York: Cambridge University Press)

Tibor Machan, ed, *The Libertarian Reader* (Rowman & Littlefield, 1982)

Erik Mack, "Individualism, Rights, and the Open Society," in *The Libertarian Reader*, Tibor Machan, ed. (Rowman & Littlefield, 1982) and several articles published in "The Personalist" in early 1970s

Herbert Marcuse, *One-Dimensional Man: Studies in the Ideology of Advanced Industrial Society* (Boston: Beacon Press, 1964)

Ludwig van Mises, *Human Action*; *Socialism*; and "Market versus Bureaucratic Planning" in *The Libertarian Reader*, Tibor Machan, ed. (Rowman & Littlefield, 1982)

Charles Murray, *Losing Ground: American Social Policy 1950-1980* (New York: Basic Books, 1986)

Gilbert Murray, *The Meaning of Freedom*, forward by Lord Samuel (London: Phaidon Press Limited, 1957)

Luis E. Navia, with Eugene Kelly, editors, *Ethics and the Search for Values* (Buffalo: Prometheus Books, 1980)

Albert J. Nock, *Our Enemy, The State* (Delevan WI: Hallberg Publishing Corp., 1983) and *On Doing the Right Thing and Other Essays* (New York: Harper & Brothers, 1928)

William F. O'Neill, *With Charity Toward None*, a critique of Objectivism (New York: Philosophical Library Inc., 1971)

Thomas Paine, "Common Sense," "The Rights of Man," and "Agrarian Justice", in *John Dos Passos presents the Living Thoughts of Tom Paine* (New York: Fawcett Publishers, 1963)

Robert W. Poole, Jr., ed., *Instead of Regulation* (Reason Foundation, 2716 Ocean Park Blvd., Suite 1062, Santa Monica CA, 90405 - 1st printing in 1984)

Ayn Rand, "The Objectivist Newsletter," (1962-1968); *Capitalism: The Unknown Ideal*, *For The New Intellectual*, and *The Virtue of Selfishness* (New York: The New American Library, 1967, 1964, and 1961)

Jean Raspail, *In the Camp of the Saints* (New York: Charles Scribners' Sons, 1975)

Douglas Rasmussen, "Essentialism, Values and Rights," in *The Libertarian Reader*, Tibor Machan, ed., (Rowman & Littlefield, 1982); and *The Philosophic Thought of Ayn Rand* with Den Uyl

Jean-François Revel, *Without Marx or Jesus* (Garden City NY: Doubleday, 1971)

Robert J. Ringer, *Restoring the American Dream* (New York: Fawcett Crest Books, 1980)

Murray Rothbard, *The Ethics of Liberty* (Atlantic Highlands NY: Humanities Press); *For a New Liberty*: A Libertarian Manifesto (New York: McMillan); and *Man, Economy, and State* (New York: NYU Press)

Alexander Rustow, *Freedom and Domination*: A Historical Critique of Civilization (Princeton: Princeton University Press)

Thomas Sowell, *Marxism: A Philosophy and Economics* and *The Economics and Politics of Race* (New York: William Morrow); *Knowledge and Decisions* (New York: Basic Books)

Morris and Linda Tannehill, *The Market For Liberty* (New York: Laissez Faire Books, Inc, 1984)

Henry David Thoreau, "Civil Disobedience," in *The Annotated Walden*, Philip van Doren Stern, ed. (New York: Clarkson N. Potter, 1970)

Henry B. Veatch, *Rational Man* (Bloomington: Indiana University Press, 1962)

John Vaizey, *Capitalism* (New York & Washington: Praeger, 1971)

Wilhelm Windelband, *A History of Philosophy*, Volumes I-III (Westport: Greenwood Press)

Garry Wills, *Inventing America* (New York: Random House); *Confessions of a Conservative* (New York: Doubleday, 1979); and "The Convenient State" from *What Is Conservatism?*, Frank S. Meyer, ed. (New York: Holt, Rinehart & Winston, 1964)

Gordon S. Wood, *The Creation of the American Republic, 1776-1787* (New York: The Norton Library, 1969)